T0360844

# Innovation in Africa

This book emphasizes the need for promoting innovation on the African continent. It identifies the roadblocks for entrepreneurs and discusses ways for developing an ecosystem for innovators to pave a way through the barriers and create ground-breaking products and new technologies which will meet consumers' needs in Africa.

In order to stimulate innovation in African countries, there is the need for a more appropriate approach for innovation to occur in a context of international openness to knowledge. This book adopts a practical approach, demonstrating how innovation is an important driver of economic growth and competitiveness. It shows that innovation in Africa should be driven by local people, in response to local problems, and that open technology and knowledge sharing are vital to this project. It further explores key enablers such as the discovery of innovative talent, overcoming barriers, building strategic partnerships and promoting innovation across the continent. The book places emphasis on the creation of an innovation ecosystem as a value-creating tool by stakeholders for nation building and growth in Africa.

This book will be of interest to researchers, students, international agencies, governments, businesses and individuals interested in the field of innovation and its potentials. It will also be relevant to investors, manufacturers and other stakeholders involved in the economic development of Africa.

**Deseye Umurhohwo** is the founder of Innovate4Africa, an initiative focused on innovation promotion. As a business consultant, she offers professional advice on innovation, strategy and corporate entrepreneurship for businesses and organizations offering solutions that will help them survive and sustain their performance. She is also engaged in the discovery and development of innovative talents leveraging on her two-decade administrative experience.

# Routledge Focus on Business and Management

The fields of business and management have grown exponentially as areas of research and education. This growth presents challenges for readers trying to keep up with the latest important insights. Routledge Focus on Business and Management presents small books on big topics and how they intersect with the world of business research.

Individually, each title in the series provides coverage of a key academic topic, whilst collectively, the series forms a comprehensive collection across the business disciplines.

**Cultural Proximity and Organization**
*Managing Diversity and Innovation*
*Federica Ceci and Francesca Masciarelli*

**Entrepreneurial Urban Regeneration**
*Business Improvement Districts as a Form of Organizational Innovation*
*Rezart Prifti and Fatma Jaupi*

**Strategic University Management**
Future Proofing Your Institution
*Loren Falkenberg and M. Elizabeth Cannon*

**Innovation in Africa**
Fuelling an Entrepreneurial Ecosystem for Growth and Prosperity
*Deseye Umurhohwo*

For more information about this series, please visit: www.routledge.com/ Routledge-Focus-on-Business-and-Management/book-series/FBM

# Innovation in Africa

Fuelling an Entrepreneurial
Ecosystem for Growth and
Prosperity

**Deseye Umurhohwo**

Taylor & Francis Group

LONDON AND NEW YORK

First published 2021
by Routledge
2 Park Square, Milton Park, Abingdon, Oxon OX14 4RN

and by Routledge
52 Vanderbilt Avenue, New York, NY 10017

*Routledge is an imprint of the Taylor & Francis Group, an informa business*

*British Library Cataloguing-in-Publication Data*
A catalogue record for this book is available from the British Library

*Library of Congress Cataloging-in-Publication Data*
A catalog record has been requested for this book

ISBN: 978-0-367-49600-5 (hbk)
ISBN: 978-1-003-04682-0 (ebk)

Typeset in Times New Roman
by codeMantra

# Contents

*Acknowledgements*                                                                vii

**1   Innovation in today's world**                                                 1
*The value of innovation  1*
*Sustaining competitive advantage with innovation  2*
*The new business environment  3*
*Embracing innovative solutions  5*
*Looking ahead  8*
*Conclusion  10*

**2   Discovering our innovative talent**                                          14
*Customers' transformation  14*
*Discovering creativity  15*
*Ideas creation  16*
*Building talents through synergy  18*
*Creativity and the success of firms  20*
*Creativity in innovation development  21*
*Imbibing creativity  24*

**3   Overcoming barriers to innovation**                                          28
*Introduction  28*
*The importance of resources  29*
*Barriers to innovation  30*
*Overcoming innovation barriers  33*
*Conclusion  37*

**4 Strategic partnerships** 41

*Introduction 41*
*Networks, knowledge and innovation 42*
*Innovation at the grassroots 44*
*Sustaining competitive advantage through*
*  strategic alliances 45*
*Engaging in networks 48*
*Building partnerships for innovation development 52*
*Conclusion 54*

**5 Promoting innovation in our environment** 60

*Adopting transformational innovation 60*
*Learning for success 62*
*Innovation stakeholders 65*
*Stakeholders' engagement strategies 68*
*Innovation promotion 70*
*Conclusion 75*

**6 Taking the next steps** 80

*Introduction 80*
*Economic development and competition 80*
*Driving innovation 82*
*Open innovation systems and knowledge sharing 84*
*The role of partnerships 86*
*Conclusion 87*

*References* 91
*Index* 109

# Acknowledgements

The inspiration to write this book is divine. I want to first thank God for helping me put my thoughts together and giving me the Grace to finish this book. I also want to appreciate my husband, Albert for his immeasurable support all through this work. The inquisitiveness of my kids, Ruemu, Yore and Kevwe contributed in one way or the other to this work. I am also grateful to my mum, Helena Oye for her underlining support and my siblings, particularly my internal motivator, Cynthia Oye-Isang.

I want to also thank my mentor, Professor Daphne Halkias for her professional support and encouragement. ISM librarian, Judy Knight, thank you for being there and for your prompt response to all enquires. I appreciate and recognise Prof. Ivo Pezzuto, for igniting my passion to promote innovation. To everyone who in one way or the other supported me, I recognise and thank you.

# 1 Innovation in today's world

## The value of innovation

The enormous contribution of innovation to value creation and development in various fields has increased the interest in the subject amongst people, businesses, institutions and nations.[1] Incontestably, it has been widely recognised as a means of securing competitive advantage and growth.[2] With a competitive world environment, organisations today are persistently determined to outperform one another with the intent of increasing their customer base.[3] As a result of the overriding importance of innovation in the corporate world, it has been labelled as the silver bullet that will secure the sustainable competitive advantage and growth of firms.[4] The greatest economic value comes from innovations that directly impact customers' use[5]; therefore, the long term survival and prosperity of firms cannot be discussed without stressing emphasising the important role of innovation.[6]

The origin of the innovation theory, recognised as the driving force behind commercial profit and economic growth which would bring about the wealth of society, was put together by Joseph Schumpeter.[7] Other perspectives of the innovation concept highlight its role in generating economic development[8] and the determination of the continued existence of an enterprise[9] in an uncertain world.[10] Prior to the extensive use of the term under consideration, processes that are associated with it and technological revolution were perceived as important.[11]

An innovation is an idea, device, process or something that can be interjected into the market and as a consequence meets new requirements, existing market needs or undisclosed desires of customers.[12] The importance of applying innovation across firms of all sizes is emphasised in another description of the word.[13] Another classification of the term under reference refers to it as the process of making changes.[14] At the centre of the definition of innovation is novelty, which is its distinctive feature.[15] This can be in the form of enhanced products, processes and routine of management. Although the word, novelty, does not satisfactorily typify innovation, the basis of the concept is the value that the innovative product generates when compared to existing solutions.[16]

Innovation is known to bring about a difference in value,[17] while the level of usefulness is significantly dependent on the judgement of the product user.[18] Viewed from another perspective, customers will perceive a product or service as an innovation if the performance exceeds something they had previously experienced.[19] An obvious stance of the subject in question sees it as a dynamic process that constantly responds to the changing needs of customers and concurrently adapts frequently to the external pressures in the competitive landscape.[20]

## Sustaining competitive advantage with innovation

In the last few decades, there have been several debates about the importance of competition and innovation across the world. Certainly, innovation represents one of the bases of competition and requires improvements together with investments in various industries in areas such as Research and Development (R&D).[21] Within a system, innovation can occur at different levels. At the functional level, it can come by way of improvements, while at the corporate level, it can take the form of new products and services, and business models. Technological breakthroughs, on the other hand, are ascribed as innovation at the level of the industry.[22] Given that innovation has been acknowledged as a core renewal process in an organisation,[23] executives have consequently realised that it is only through the creation of new products and services, in addition to practices and processes, that their companies would continue to grow and flourish.[24]

The need to examine innovation as a solution for securing competitive advantage and growth[25] should therefore not be overlooked. We cannot also muse over the survival of companies without bringing to the fore factors that give them a competitive advantage. This brings us to the related concept of business innovation. From a definition standpoint, the notion of business innovation is described as new ideas or solutions that create business value and increases the competitive advantage of a firm.[26] The changing world we live in today requires businesses to satisfy customer needs using innovative products they have created.[27] Meanwhile, the competitiveness of most organisations is underlined by their innovative capabilities which include their innate abilities, processes and services that increases value for customers.[28]

There are several interpretations and forms of innovation which bring to light its importance in transforming an uncertain world.[29]

Broadly, there are two types, namely incremental and disruptive. The continuous improvement of features of existing products is known as incremental innovation.[30] This form of innovation is also characterised by the extension of current organisational capabilities.[31] Further description of incremental innovation shows that it is a situation where there is a slight improvement in available technology.[32] This can also be in the form of upgrade of a product design or process, without a fundamental advancement or acquisition of new machinery.[33] In real terms, what this demonstrates is that with continuous improvement, the substantial elements of products can be improved upon.[34] Usually incremental innovations can occur from practice[35] while the distinction in the value of a new product is evident when it is weighed against an existing one.[36] another interpretation of the subject shows that for organisations, the implementation of new methods related to the business operations is measured as incremental innovation and can be in areas such as supply chain management and quality control. What is more, the resolution of management on matters concerning the relationship with external bodies and the restructuring of authority fall under the aforementioned type of innovation.[37]

On the other hand, innovations that are disruptive or radical start with simple or uncomplicated applications and gradually build up to displace well-known brands of competitors in due course.[38] They can also be described as a new combination of performance features, entirely new products, or the result of a major decline in costs.[39] Radical innovations are further expressed as the disruption of existing industry capacities as a result of new knowledge and skills.[40] It should be pointed out that novel products from revolutionary innovation can result from advances in knowledge and technology.[41] The effect of disruptive innovation can be seen in the example of Japanese industries at a point in time, when the concept under reference, brought about a phenomenal growth in the country with the launch of cheap photocopiers by Canon in the market, and eventually disrupted Xerox's established models.[42] Overall, innovation is considered as a propellant for business growth and prosperity[43]; therefore, organisations need to engage in this activity with the aim of renewing the value of their assets.[44]

## The new business environment

There are other forms of innovation that give us a better understanding of the subject. What we commonly have in small firms what we commonly have is non-technological innovation which can be in the form of superior packaging of products, or the opening of new outlets for selling goods.[45] Innovations that are non-technological can also be in the form of alterations in the presentation of goods, or the launch of a new pricing system.[46] Relatedly, technical innovation is described as the indirect creation of value by way of adjustment of processes and performance, whilst the focus of marketing innovation is on the introduction of strategies such as the implementation of a sales promotion.[47] The focus of a different perspective of the concept is the fundamental improvement in the value and appearance of products for the benefit of customers.[48] There are other classifications of innovation that are drawn from varying scales of teams, departments and professional disciplines, making the subject an area of concern for practitioners and researchers across a range of business and management disciplines.[49]

Other than the definition, it is necessary to draw attention to the significance of innovation, which is centred on the process of creating outstanding value for customers, especially when they are considered the most important part of the value chain.[50] The aforesaid underlines the strategic role of the customer in defining a product.[51] Since the real goal of innovation is to turn an idea into something valuable for the business,[52] the worth of an innovation essentially is determined by the business context and not[53] by the mere allocation of a commercial value to an idea.[54] Viewed differently, it is not only the proprietors of the company that define a product; on the contrary, other stakeholders such as customers, and society are equally important in classifying a product. A more appropriate approach of considering the value of products therefore is not by scrutinising the product itself, but by also taking into cognizance its effect as mentioned above.[55]

Ideally, in determining the characteristic of an innovative product, it is necessary to understand the difference between the new product and the one that existed previously.[56] Surely, looking beyond a product is a good way of determining its innovative character, but what is required is to take into account the activity that stem from the interaction between the product and the stakeholders within a context.[57] An innovative product induces positive effect when measured in relation to the goals of the company, consumers and the society. This positive effect can be based on three dimensions, namely appropriateness, valuable and desirability.[58]

Over the years, the role of innovation in the area of service provision has become apparent. Services are interpreted as mixed concepts where each one is exclusive and cannot be totally replicated.[59] In line with this description, service innovations are expressed in terms of the value created through offers delivered. It is important to mention that distinct services are known to emanate from the contribution of people to the domain of knowledge.[60] They are also regarded as the process in which an enterprise carries out changes in its culture, procedures and operations, with the aim of adding value to the outcome of their service for customers' benefit.[61] A further interest of innovation in services is the generation of added and future value, through incremental and radical services, respectively.[62] Irrespective of where technology leads, it should be recognised that service differentiation comes from people and their contribution to the infinite field of knowledge.[63]

From the resource-based perspective, value creation can be seen from the standpoint of using manifested proficient resources[64] to create and capture value.[65] Consequently, in an effort to satisfy needs, innovative products will have to be produced.[66] The search for value creation using appropriate service concepts is what radical innovation service is all about.[67] For Incremental innovations, they can be combined and replicated to solve problems of customers[68] and the value created from delivering the new service would bring about benefits for the organisation.[69] Beyond a firm's technological innovation, the concept of value creation has increasingly become important.[70]

The nature of competition today has changed as it is now being redefined by timeframe. With this transformation, speed has become essential while product cycles are getting shorter. At the same time, development times are becoming tighter, with customers expecting almost instantaneous service.[71] In the light of the above, the focus and attention of firms offering services should be on thrilling customers with creativity and innovation in their offerings.[72] An extended version of the concept of innovation in the service industry in operational terms is the anticipation of firms to think for customers and offer enhanced value to them.[73] As a dynamic process that constantly responds to the changing needs of clients, innovation is known to frequently adapt to the external uproar in the competitive landscape.[74] It is also connected with the execution of business techniques in organisations such as internal management and the interface with external bodies.[75]

## Embracing innovative solutions

Indisputably, the role of technology in our lives is apparent. It has played a critical role in time past, and also shaped the way things are today. Undoubtedly, technology will continue to do more in the future.[76] Technological innovation is innermost in the economic growth and enhancement of efficiency,[77] particularly in the prompt and proficient development of products and services.[78] The concept of value in technological innovation, however, is not straight plain to a certain extent but more accurately measured by changes in performance and procedures.[79]

The preceding paragraphs have established that innovation and technological advancement are imperative for an enduring economic growth and livelihood[80]; hence, they cannot be avoided by any business organisation desirous of sustaining competitive advantage in the market.[81] Although the study of the impact of innovation on economic performance has been partially neglected in the mainstream economies,[82] the strong link between economic growth and technological innovation has been outlined by many experts.[83] As a result, there has been an increasing necessity for efficiency and value product development in a technologically ambitious world.[84] Noticeable innovations such as electric power trains, airplanes, computers and others are the upshot of a multitude of less visible technological improvements than the earlier versions which were often very crude and primitive.[85] Without a doubt, the internet has facilitated access to the global marketplace with the absence of border confinements. It is considered as a flexible expansion of a firm's aptitude, with human imagination being the only constraint in the environment.[86]

From the articulated definitions, we can appreciate the value of innovation. Those that bring about economic significance are classified to be related to the specific impact on consumers' value.[87] The whole essence of the concept under reference is the generation of outstanding service for the benefit of the consumer.[88] From the perspective of the business framework, the significance of innovation is established and highlighted instead of the allotment of money-making value to a conceived idea.[89] It must be recognised that new ideas are the seeds for economic growth and they increase a firm's efficiency. Nevertheless, the extent to which this occurs depends on the closeness of the idea to the company's technological position.[90]

As a matter of fact, the rise in living standards is dependent on the effectiveness of transforming new ideas into consumer products or production processes. Converting an idea into a product, or converting the production process is by no means immediate. The implementation of the above requires someone with a vision, or application and expertise, to bring it to reality.[91] Ideally, generated ideas that are not used by the company can be traded off.[92] In developing new products therefore, companies should not concentrate on the definition of the product; rather, their attention should be on the effect that the product advances.[93] The example of MYSQL (the world's leading open-source database software company) can be used to illustrate the earlier point made. The company was more interested in increasing the number of users and developers than in generating revenue. The consequence of the action of the founders led to a value creating system with over 10 million clients as well as several co-creators designing new elements and evaluating the software.[94]

The 21st-century business world has witnessed an astounding rate of transformation in the economy, with an emphasised need for firms to innovate or be overthrown! Certainly, this will not come easy as existing protocols are built on the conviction of durability while the controls on hand are established on the exploration of confidence. Meanwhile, at the workplace, human resources guidelines have been set up on the supposition of homogeneity in the labour force, whereas the mindsets of workers are influenced by yesterday's success. Clearly, the listed strengths collectively act as a major source of inaction. Innovation in this circumstance would therefore be seen as endangering current procedures, controls, policies and more essentially the frame of mind, because the incidents that brought about a company's greatness may no longer be the same.[95] In addition to the anticipatory action to be in charge, organisations have been modified by innovation, in reaction to the changes in the external environment.[96] Hence, the innovativeness of a product is determined by the actions that emerge from the correlation between products and stakeholders.[97] In the face of market challenges, companies should not focus on the classification of products; rather, attention should be on the impact on customers.[98]

An interesting event in recent times which individuals and companies across industries should take note of is the proliferation and use of software.[99] Undeniably, a number of businesses and industries are being operated on software, which is being delivered effectively using innovation. Amazon, a foremost bookseller with the aptitude for selling everything online, is a good example of a software company to cite.[100] Disney is another company that has also successfully applied software in its entertainment business. The company acquired Pixar to retain relevance in animated movies.[101] The financial service industry has also been visibly transformed by software, with virtually every transaction ranging from $1 to millions of dollars being carried out using software. Remarkably, many of the innovators in the financial services sector, are software companies, such as Square, which facilitates payments using mobile devices and applications providing the service called *Paywith Square*. There is also PayPal in the above mentioned category.[102] Banking systems also as a result of the rapid global competition and structural change, have resorted to the use of new technology.

With the increasing expectations of their teeming customers, they have sought to develop and implement service innovations in their organisations.[103] Photography has definitely been dominated and taken over by software. Virtually all mobile phones today have software-powered cameras with capacity of uploading and archiving pictures on devices and channels.[104] In some industries, the software revolution is principally an opportunity for incumbents. In next to no time, new software ideas will result in the rise of start-ups, similar to Silicon Valley. The impending contest between incumbents and software-powered disruptors in the future will be quite ambitious.[105]

In every industry, firms must realise that the software revolution is imminent. There are instances where incumbent leaders such as Oracle and Microsoft are threatened by new software offerings like Salesforce.com and Android.[106] Telecommunications, aviation, logistics and defence are amongst several other industries where the influence of software is evident.[107] In the light of the above, the need to acknowledge and take the challenge of the software transformation by organisations is the way to go.[108] The new competitive approach is that the source code of the software is freely available to everybody to use and modify as appropriate.[109]

## Looking ahead

Opportunities in the area of human activity are essential for innovation, as they provide the capabilities for it to occur.[110] There are prospects for individuals with knowledge to stand on as channels of bringing forth innovations[111], it is necessary at this point to consider the important role of competition. In several organisations, besides the value created for customers, competition is highlighted by the capabilities and proficiency that point in the right direction.[112] Nonetheless, when the performance of a product or service exceeds the existing experience of a customer, it is perceived as innovation.[113] With increased competition and rapid transformation, small and medium sized enterprises can influence greatly the present market economy.[114] The fiscal and technological growth of many countries will be enhanced through the innovative potentials in new products and processes.[115] Consequently, the renewal in an innovation should involve components that can be replicated in new situations.[116]

We can discern from the competitive environment if the innovation process is a functional one by its steady response to the changing requirements of customers and adjustments to the external unsteadiness in the environment.[117] Other related factors for consideration include retaining a competitive advantage in the market.[118]

Innovations targeted at low income earners are those that challenge cost and offer cheap goods and services.[119] the group in question group yearns for innovations that match their needs. The Tata Group Nano car is a classic example of an innovative product, created with people at the bottom of the pyramid in mind. For the company to successfully achieve this, it had to re-engineer and re-design the process of manufacturing this vehicle for the targeted market.[120] The supplier strategy was also redefined to focus on outsourcing a huge portion of the vehicle's parts while a limited number of vendors were engaged to attain reduced transaction costs.[121] The innovation strategy implemented by the above-mentioned company, created new growth opportunities in other dominant markets in America and Europe. In reaction, existing firms in the industry had to opt for less skilled personnel to carry out the responsibility of expensive specialists.[122] The above outline shows that the low income attribute of the Bottom of the Pyramid will demand innovations that address cost concerns and offer inexpensive goods and services.[123]

Clearly, knowledge and experience are used to discover innovation. Although it is prompted by needs, our experience with the product however helps to process information. The more we engage with a product, service or process, the better we can appreciate its performance and ascertain the degree of innovativeness. Sometimes, an inconsequential improvement can be considered as innovative, provided it meets our needs.[124]

Given that innovations are generated from ideas, they can be described as inspirations that should be translated into reality; otherwise, they would remain as thoughts.[125] Company employees are known to also contribute their ideas to innovations that have transformed their organisations.[126] On its own, idea generation is okay, but this action should not come before a foremost need is identified. Individuals and companies can distinguish themselves from competitors by determining first the needs of customers, and not get comfortable with just generating ideas.[127]

The point to take from the above is that the demand for innovation thrives all around us.[128] Innovations that are initiated from the needs of customers are deemed to be more successful because they have a definite purpose and reason for their existence.[129] Clearly, no organisation or individual can realise all customers' aspirations. Innovation starts with a fulfilled need or flows from overlooked necessities and its development is[130] dependent on the composite strength of the innovation[131] which has the capability of creating the new and damaging the old![132]

## Conclusion

The obvious contribution of innovation can be seen in the modifications of offers and the way business models and operations have been transformed.[133] The *Walkman* is an appropriate example to demonstrate how innovation can change markets. Developed with the capability of creating a musical environment for the individual in public, this device enabled the user to enjoy the pleasure of music without being limited to a specific location. The success of the product paved the way for the introduction of other creative consumer electronics such as mobile phones and further opened new markets for miniature and handy devices, in line with the associated lifestyle and identity of users.[134] Having established the importance of innovation in our economy, the consideration of the consequences of innovation with regards to economic performance and transformation should not be ignored.[135] With every newly implemented solution, useful problems are discovered, thereby making the process a circular one.[136] Companies are well aware that they have to develop and offer new and innovative products in order to survive and take on greater environmental and social responsibility attached to the effect of their products. This poses a challenge on the way we perceive innovative products, and calls for a better understanding of the socio-technical system a product becomes part of.[137]

In the quest for growth, individuals, firms and nations are required to think about innovation as a principal source of wealth creation.[138] Evidently, the continued existence of companies in the 21st century and beyond cannot be planned without the consideration of critical issues that give them a competitive advantage.[139] Despite the broad acceptance of the centrality of innovation, many enterprises still encounter difficulties in their endeavours.[140] On the other hand, the development and implementation of disruptive innovation are not well understood,[141] and only a small number of companies manage to leverage and maximise their capabilities in this area.[142]

Overall, there is a general presupposition that institutions are capable of stimulating innovation towards economic growth. In order to achieve this, the relevant institutions will be required. Without a doubt, the adoption of the aforementioned in developing countries can bring about the much desired accelerated growth.[143] Everything considered, if there are still reservations about the usefulness and application of innovation in companies today, one only needs to check the chances of survival of firms that still operate their businesses the way they did decades ago. The answer to this question would indisputably be in the negative.[144]

## Notes

1 Meigounpoory, Rezvani and Afshar (2015).
2 Xie, Zeng and Tan (2010).
3 Urbancova (2013).
4 Huber, Kaufmann and Steinmann (2017).
5 Huber, Kaufmann and Steinmann (2017).
6 Dillon, Lee and Matheson (2005).
7 Schumpeter (1934).
8 Schumpeter (1934).
9 Drucker (1988); Christensen (1997).
10 Assink (2006).
11 Veblen (1899); Schumpeter (1934).
12 Schipper and Swets (2010).
13 Bessant and Tidd (2009).
14 O'Sullivan and Dooley (2008).
15 Lundvall (1992).
16 Tan and McAloone (2006).
17 Tan and McAloone (2006).
18 Daniels (2014).
19 McLaughlin and Caraballo (2013).
20 Helfat, Finkelstein, Mitchell, Peteraf, Siegh, Teece and Winter (2007).
21 Tan and McAloone (2006).
22 Edquist (1997).
23 Baregheh, Rowley and Sambrook (2009).
24 Gratton (2006).
25 Xie, Zeng and Tam (2010).
26 Meyer (2013).
27 Tan and McAloone (2006).
28 Assink (2006).
29 Assink (2006).
30 Watty (2013).
31 Kiely (1993).
32 Shapiro (2002).
33 Weiser (2011).
34 Jay and Ria (1999).
35 Böhmer and Lindemann (2015).
36 Tan and McAloone (2006).
37 CBS (2012).
38 Christensen (1997).
39 Romer (1986).
40 McCormick and Maalu (2011).
41 OECD (2005).
42 Meyer (2013).
43 Baiyere and Roos (2011).
44 Schumpeter (1950).
45 Peters (1997).
46 Hamel and Prahalad (1994).
47 McLaughlin and Caraballo (2013).
48 Kiely (1993).
49 Baregheh, Rowley and Sambrook (2009).

50  Dillon, Lee and Matheson (2005).
51  Tan and McAloone (2006).
52  Kiely (1993).
53  Huber, Kaufmann and Steinmann (2017).
54  Huber, Kaufmann and Steinmann (2017).
55  Adams (2005).
56  Tan and McAloone (2006).
57  Robotham and Guldbrandsen (2000).
58  Tan and McAloone (2006).
59  Assink (2006).
60  Urbancova (2013).
61  Jacobs and Zulu (2012).
62  Tinguely (2013).
63  Hamel (2003).
64  Kandampully (2002).
65  Hamel (2003).
66  Hamel (2003).
67  Tan and McAloone (2006).
68  Urbancova (2013).
69  Assink (2006).
70  Sundbo and Gallouj (2000).
71  Schumpeter (1934).
72  Hamel and Prahalad (1994).
73  Tinguely (2013).
74  Kandampully (2002).
75  Peters (1997).
76  Central Bureau Statistics (2012).
77  Tan and McAloone (2006).
78  Tinguely (2013).
79  Johnson and Kirchain (2011).
80  Urbancova (2013).
81  McLaughlin and Caraballo (2013).
82  Tinguely (2013).
83  Tinguely (2013).
84  Porter and Stern (2001).
85  Kline and Rosenberg (1986).
86  Krugman (1994).
87  Nelson and Winter (1977).
88  Assink (2006).
89  Cantwell (2005).
90  Basadur (2004).
91  Eyal-Cohen (2019).
92  Cantwell (2005).
93  Tinguely (2013).
94  Urbancova (2013).
95  Aghion, Howitt and Bursztyn (2010).
96  Xie, Zeng and Tam (2010).
97  Baker and Sinkula (2002).
98  Robotham and Guldbrandsen (2000).
99  Robotham and Guldbrandsen (2000).

100 Ojeaga (2015).
101 Harel, Schwartz and Kaufmann (2019).
102 Andreessen (2011).
103 Andreessen (2011).
104 Assink (2006).
105 Andreessen (2011).
106 Andreessen (2011).
107 Andreessen (2011).
108 Andreessen (2011).
109 Andreessen (2011).
110 Assink (2006).
111 Kooskora(2004).
112 Assink (2006).
113 Adams (2005).
114 Coulson-Thomas (2012).
115 Shapiro (2002).
116 Hippel (2005).
117 Assink (2006).
118 Urbancova (2013).
119 Urbancova (2013).
120 Baiyere and Roos (2011).
121 Baiyere and Roos (2011).
122 Wentz (2010).
123 Baiyere and Roos (2011).
124 Baiyere and Roos (2011).
125 Meyer (2013).
126 Basadur (2004).
127 Eyal-Cohen (2019).
128 Huber, Kaufmann and Steinmann (2017).
129 Karlsson and Törlind (2013).
130 Amabile (1998).
131 Baker and Sinkula (2002).
132 Huber, Kaufmann and Steinmann (2017).
133 Meyer (2013).
134 Tan and McAloone (2006).
135 Meyer (2013).
136 Meyer (2013).
137 Assink (2006).
138 Huber, Kaufmann and Steinmann (2017).
139 Meyer (2013).
140 Huber, Kaufmann and Steinmann (2017).
141 Leifer (2001).
142 Assink (2006).
143 Oyelaran-Oyeyinka, Laditan and Esubiyi (1996).
144 Tinguely (2013).

# 2 Discovering our innovative talent

## Customers' transformation

With the transformation in consumers' lifestyles and the never-ending increase in their demand for an assortment of products,[1] there has been a corresponding rising need for innovation by organisations. These changes in consumers' needs have presented numerous opportunities in the marketplace for companies to take advantage of.[2] In adapting to the competitive environment, firms are required to envision themselves as customers and also act on their behalf by introducing products and services they will need in the future. The implementation of this step demonstrates the act of anticipating an upcoming reality.[3] Thinking on behalf of the customer requires an enterprise to have the important skill of forecasting. Once needs are identified, ideas are then sought and after that creativity begins.[4] The power of anticipation is very timely in the promotion of innovation. It is what distinguishes an outstanding performance in the area of business and other fields such as sports.[5] This brings to the fore the point that innovation can occur at any time and at various levels, and more importantly, the essence that it should be driven by needs.[6]

Creativity is recognised as a critical function of innovation; therefore it is important to discuss its role and influence for a better understanding of how we should incorporate this skill in our lives and business activities. The development of the personality traits of individuals and the influence of an organisation's structure on its growth has a correlation to the generation of innovative ideas and creativity.[7] For this reason the background and factors in which individuals act, to a large extent, ascertain their entrepreneurial personality.[8] The act to create should not be estimated but habitually displayed and be allowed to flow instinctively just like kids. By nature, children are explorative,[9] and they imaginatively change their playing rules as often as they like, as they get tired.[10]

## Discovering creativity

The call for creativity to be sustained is more than ever before emphasised. A functional precondition for this, however, is for the individual to have an open attitude towards new ideas, a taste for substitute solutions and an inclination to undertake risks.[11] Stimulating, creativity in individuals and organisations can be done by engaging in certain activities such as problem solving and fabrication of machines. The outcome of designed items should thereafter be shared with others. The role of communication skills is critical here as they will enhance the possible attainment of the problem-solving objectives.[12]

Another means of unbolting individuals' resourcefulness is by inspiring valuable attributes like inquisitiveness and responsiveness.[13] These qualities are considered central to discovering creative talents and at the same time will help us change the way we envision things and cope with failure.[14] Interestingly, the above-mentioned character of inquisitiveness is reliable in distinguishing those that can transform a culture.[15] Overall, individual factors and the background in which they act can be used to ascertain their entrepreneurial personality.[16] Some ingenious persons, although not entrepreneurs, have contributed to general knowledge that can be used and accessed by other agents to create new products and processes. The implication of this is that entrepreneurial opportunities can be objective and may not necessarily be the outcome of the creativity of the entrepreneur.[17] In view of the aforesaid, it is important that we optimise our creative potentials. Achieving this requires balancing the strength and extent of our knowledge.[18] It further requires working in partnership with people of different intellect foundations with spotlight on building up the individual's intellectual position.[19]

In addition, to develop the creative skill calls for critical and analytical thinking. These abilities signify the competence to judge how valuable a person's idea is. It also assesses the advantages and disadvantages of ideas and further suggests ways of advancing them. By application, critical thinking is the capability to exploit intellectual skills in everyday circumstances apart from trading creative ideas.[20] Some key aspects of the concept under reference are testing solutions that deviate from the status quo and remaining calm when these solutions differ from established ones.[21] It is important to mention also that disparity in opinions is a healthy requirement for innovation to thrive because it supports consultations.[22] The necessity of creativity in the quest to promote innovation is critical. Hence, unleashing our creative confidence at this point is an appropriate action. Corporate

policy, consequently, should consciously promote and encourage curiosity amongst individuals, just as teams are required to engage in
problem-solving activities and learning. For successful outcomes,
some elements including time, dedication and openness to all types of
ideas are essential.[23]

Competition is one aspect that should be considered in the
innovation journey. It is a factor that determines the success or failure of a firm. The nature of competition and the actors have over
time changed in line with adjustments in customers' expectations.[24]
Closely related to the above is the prevailing concept of decreasing
product life cycle.[25] With this reality, it has become crucial for firms
to concentrate more on innovation. Besides this, they still need to in-
fuse flexibility in their operations and management.[26] In the light of
the aforementioned, companies cannot run away from organisational
transformation which involves the redistribution of resources and
the development of talents. Other aspects of competition are planning, product collection and process modification.[27] For firms and
businesses to sustain their leadership positions, they would have to
continue to innovate and surpass their rivals for the benefit of their
customers.[28]

Business problems are sometimes complex and because of their
peculiar characteristics, they cannot be resolved using regular solutions. Though the use of standard solutions can be applicable in solving simple and intricate problems, what is required to unravel complex
problems are creative problem-solving skills.[29] Applicably, future innovations are expected to come from the effective combination of components.[30] What counts for businesses is the ability to innovate and the
potential of generating creative results.[31]

There is need to also highlight the function of the system which is the
capacity of the firm to constantly convert knowledge and ideas into offerings for the advantage of customers and other stakeholders.[32] To ac-
tualise this, individuals and enterprises are encouraged to be open and
acquiescent to new ideas.[33] Since the conception of brilliant initiatives
can sometimes be time-consuming, it should be appropriately applied
to the general promotion of innovation and not just in the direction of
new products' production.[34]

## Ideas creation

A critical look at the innovation process reveals that individuals are
at the hub of the course. They create ideas that can ignite solutions,
expand technology and generate products and services.[35] This point
is attested to, by many who agree that innovation is initiated by ideas

that are captured in coordinated programmes. For valuable insights, assumptions made should go beyond the specialty of firms and take the approach of diverse viewpoints.[36] Without doubt, being receptive to new ideas is a precondition for the formation of an innovative culture for this reason it is important for teams and management to adopt this skill.[37] Sometimes, certain initiatives produced go untested especially when needs are not identified or prompted.[38]

A relevant question that is often asked is, *how are ideas developed*? In giving an answer, it is vital to point out that ideas generation should be supplemented by structured gathering of information.[39]

Basically, there are at least two phases involved in creating ideas. The first phase is concerned with interest while the second is centred on the promotion of the idea. Everything about the content of the idea is what the first stage is about while the second stage is focused on the support of the idea by an individual.[40] Once ideas have been successfully generated in the first step they should be pruned down to a manageable number for further development at the next stage of the process.[41] At this level, there are three steps to be considered. The first step is the ideation process where different creative methods are applied. This is closely followed by the evaluation and selection phases. Here, ideas selected are streamlined for further deliberations and processing.[42] Usually, ideas from the earlier process without definite needs are not marketable.[43] However, it is essential to keep in mind that moving ideas from the conception to the completion stage requires a determined mindset.[44]

Open innovation has been recognised as another source that triggers the generation of viable ideas. Using this concept, forwarded ideas are evaluated and filtered based on principles such as business strategy.[45] The shortlisted initiatives from the evaluation and sorting processes are thereafter adopted as a project by the management of the organisation. Discarded ideas may be due to certain factors including those related to content or policy.[46] In the course of disposing unwanted ideas however, attention should be given to novel ideas with disruptive characteristics and prospects for success. The above-mentioned concern is timely as some radical ideas are regrettably abandoned sometimes.[47] Generating viable ideas can also occur when individuals participate in leisure activities because they provide an opportunity for them to reflect on new thoughts. There is a similar notion that ideas can be generated during tranquil moods in a different environment from the one we are familiar with. Once the ideas are generated, it may be necessary sometimes for them to go through an incubation stage for inclusion and collation of diverse thoughts and views.[48]

More often than not, ideas are considered to emerge from a connection of existing knowledge. As earlier stated, the attainment of appropriate information is a critical part of this process.[49] The tendency of individuals to create innovative solutions is said to be an indication of the outcome of their creativity and their position in relation to the flow of information.[50] The advice is for individuals to be engaged in several ways of thinking and portraying their created ideas in several forms. The focus of the earlier point made is on the transmission of conceptual ideas through the exploration of material objects and events.[51] Despite the importance attached to idea creation, on their own, ideas will remain inconsequential until they are matched with a human need. The effect of this statement is that at the point where innovation is tied to a need is when we can say it has been initiated.[52]

From observation, some initiatives with great potentials are sometimes abandoned, while the flow of productive thinking is also shut down hurriedly.[53] Few people on their part are not interested in looking out for trends and prospects to unearth problems; rather they depend and wait for others to do so.[54] Introducing innovation and making it a regular routine for individuals and organisations is an identified shared goal and the recommended approach of accomplishing this task is to transform ideas into substance of value.[55] In creating a path for the future, innovators can deliver value using different methods such as testing and education. Applying this will stimulate and bring about success.[56]

## Building talents through synergy

The significance of knowledge in the innovation process is paramount because it represents a valuable contribution and an outcome of the transformation process.[57] The impact of knowledge on innovation is further highlighted[58] as an intellectual asset of the organisation. It is also utilised as part of the resources to determine the innovative capacity of the firm.[59] Further explanation of the concept in reference is its consideration as a priceless and non-physical asset that propels the connection of information in the innovation system and the major role it plays in the rapid replication of success.[60] An individual's knowledge is clearly an outcome of the interaction he has with others.[61] As a standard, knowledge offering is expected to interconnect, adapt, sort and anticipate. In the light of the above, companies in their outlook should start reflecting on how swiftly new businesses can be set up. Clearly, the reality of the times suggests that some businesses operating today may not stand at the same time.[62]

Making the best of our creative potentials calls for a balance between the strength and extent of knowledge as previously emphasised.[63] Accordingly, it has been suggested that the wits of a person can be built by working in affiliation with others.[64] Therefore, establishing a strong connection between business partners and vendors is a strategy for getting new insights. It is also a foremost avenue for the realisation of a sense of impending needs. By the same token, connecting with rivals can also enable firms to position themselves in the market. It has therefore become imperative for companies to link up with other industries and sectors at the global level, for opportunities and access to knowledge and ideas.[65] Within the enterprise, compelling competition is also capable of inspiring innovation.[66] Without a doubt, the possibilities of connections are endless.[67]

In the information age, the impact of entrepreneurship is being felt at a large scale. The consequence of this is that entrepreneurs are discovering business models that can deliver value at an increasing pace.[68] Against the backdrop of inherent advantages, they can envisage new solutions for existing customers and non-consumers.[69] Innovations are sometimes as a result of the successful formation of a collective exploit of a group, working together and the story of Apple Incorporation illustrates this point. Here, a number of people contributed to translating Apple's product to reality even though the founder of Apple, Steve Jobs, had the insight into the position and package of the product in question.[70] The approach that the company used was to create an ecosystem and work around it.[71] Indisputably, many innovations materialise because of the knack of connecting diverse technologies and new potentials. The example of the iPod demonstrates the above mentioned viewpoint. This device was created from a chain of advances by some people in the microelectronics field through a combination of software and media technologies.[72]

There are two dimensions that highlight the operation of connections. The first relates to associations and acquaintances we make with people we work with, while the other is concerned with business interest in the course of the innovators' journey.[73] Connecting with others is clearly recognised as one of the indispensable skills an individual should possess. As a basic talent, it is inherent in all of us from our early growth stage, although in varying levels. This skill however gradually fades away particularly as we become active in the competitive business environment.[74] Concerning the proficiency of firms, there is a need to emphasise that the core competencies of firms have been refined to include their ability to creatively combine skills internally and externally.[75] Without a doubt, our competitive world has brought about uncertainty, threats and risks for entrepreneurs. The effect of the foregoing on resources is that emphasis has now shifted from natural to mental.[76] To succeed therefore, innovators require guts to conquer unfamiliar territories. Active participants in the innovation process are known for putting into action a combination of new factors in the process.[77] Besides individuals, enterprises such as research and academic institutions can also help to induce innovation.[78] For individuals, concepts such as educational accomplishment(s), employment and self-confidence are linked to their innovativeness.[79] Entrepreneurs in certain locations are also said to be more susceptible to engaging in innovation-related matters.[80]

## Creativity and the success of firms

An assessment of the innovation process in firms reveals that successful outcomes rely on certain individuals who are not hindered by the limited support they receive from their organisations. The absence of this support may not be unrelated to the ineffective innovation management system being operated by these enterprises.[81] The aforesaid brings to the front the importance of uncovering innovative talent and why it is requisite for this to be achieved. Discovering innovators within teams allows for possibilities by inspiring geniuses to express their talents. The skilfulness of individuals can be discovered when competences are built in a process or system of participation. Here, team members have a chance to discover those poised for greatness.[82] In addition to talent, innovation development requires individuals and companies to develop a risk averse attitude.[83] From this standpoint of capitalising on strengths, an innovator can source for work-related information from social groups while Credence should be given to signs of progress and success in activities being engaged in.[84]

In line with building an enduring mindset for innovation, there is need for individuals to be self-sufficient in their thoughts. Achieving this requires a thorough evaluation of information in addition to overcoming standard practices, obstacles and threats.[85] With the increased responsiveness for innovation, we see[86] how committed entrepreneurs are encouraged to be open to ambiguity.[87]

As part of efforts in developing the self-esteem of innovative entrepreneurs, they should be engaged in meaningful contests and actions.[88] Potential areas where interest in innovation can be generated are product improvement contests organised for several purposes at different points, but targeted at all types of groups. In Sweden, for instance, the above activity was implemented where ideas and design contests were organised for groups. The result of the outcome brought about a change in the paradigm of the country.[89]

Motivation has an underlining value in innovation and can come in various ways. Although it can occur naturally, at institutions of learning and workplaces, the type of motivation that is applicable is described as intrinsic.[90] We also have extrinsic motivation which also plays an important role as the former determining the success or impediment of creativity. A person who is extrinsically inspired will be inclined to take the easiest and fastest path to achieve set objectives in order to obtain the reward at the end. In contrast, the intrinsically motivated person will search various options and alternatives and work at his or her pace with pleasure to resolve issues. Using the described exploration method can lead to the discovery of novel solutions, some of which may become more successful than the original findings.[91]

It has been discovered that people are more creative when they are motivated by elements such as interest, pleasure and challenge of work, and not by external pressures.[92] Further information about intrinsic motivation shows that it can be developed in formal institutions like the classroom and workplace.[93] Beyond cognitive abilities, motivational attitudes such as childhood curiosity and perseverance based on obsession will reveal individuals that can make a difference.[94] In promoting innovation therefore, it is important to search for meaningful challenges and actions that can serve as a spring to improve the self-worth of individuals towards the establishment of strength-based motivation.[95] Apart from the above-mentioned factors, education, experience and the size of an organisation are other identified characteristics that can influence innovation.[96]

## Creativity in innovation development

Today, it is unlikely for anyone to be successful without frequent improvement of his or her talent, knowledge and capacity.[97] It is noteworthy to restate here that there are different avenues that can be explored to stimulate the required talents for innovation. Asking questions regularly and searching for appropriate answers will prompt designers and entrepreneurs to discover fresh methods of tackling established processes.[98] It is equally critical to be on the watch for links, gaps and inconsistencies when trying to understand and solve problems.[99] Interestingly, difficulties experienced can sometimes stir up innovation, hence, they should not always be seen as constraints.[100] Innovations at the bottom of the pyramid markets, for instance, are determined by the way organisations fulfil the special needs of these consumers.[101]

The inclusion of innovation in a development programme will lead to the materialisation of concealed talents.[102] Other factors and activities that are considered important to improve creativity include education, experimentation and motivation. Furthermore business size and economic segments also play a role in innovation promotion.[103] With the intensified call to promote innovation in the African continent, there is need to consciously move beyond the obvious, and seek new ways to solve problems. In doing this, the pressure to search for quick solutions should be avoided, as this may not necessarily be the best option. Going beyond the initial workable idea we find should be the guiding principle in the innovation process.[104]

Another area of consideration is the effective use of resources in the innovation process. Time and money are regarded as critical resources an organisation should efficiently utilise. We can also relate time pressure to the earlier discussed subject of motivating people for increased creativity. If emphasis is placed on the urgency and sense of challenge for instance, time pressure under certain conditions can lead to improvement in creativity. However, unrealistic tight schedules can cause burnout and mistrust if they are not managed.[105] Clearly, the support received for the business operation can increase the pace of flexibility and propel management to provide the resources and confidence that will pave the way for innovation. At the same time, it will help deliver immense benefits for individuals, the organisation and the environment.[106]

The concept of a firm's capacity is closely related to the subject of resources. This capability can be judged as the most important that the firm should build on[107] because it effectively combines knowledge and the outcome will be demonstrated in innovative products, services, processes and systems.[108] Ideally, the core competence of a firm is its capacity to resourcefully combine basic skills internally and externally.[109] Viewed from another perspective, the conversion of assets into superior products and services over that of competitors', in in line with the continued competitive advantage of a firm, lies in its capability.[110] For this to be achieved, the support of top management is critical.[111]

Having discussed the resources and competencies of a firm, it is important also to focus on the need for an innovative culture as a means of facilitating creativity. The relevance of building an innovative culture is becoming apparent by the day. Having this environment will enable the expansion of combined knowledge from all fields. The environment of an innovative culture essentially considers different perspectives of a problem after reflecting and sorting diverse views of it.[112] It requires the development and sustenance of the covert abilities of individuals to build such a culture and managers have the responsibility to ensure this happens.[113] The culture at Silicon Valley is typical. Here, unsuccessful start-ups are encouraged and engaged because the failure of firms in the system is not attributed to the originators of the ideas generated. Rather, some possible explanations are given as reasons for the setback they experienced.[114]

Clearly, as a result of its contribution to the creation and attainment of a company's competitive advantage, an innovative culture is apt.[115] Again, discovering our innovative talents requires the acquisition of capabilities as a measure of sustaining our advantage in the competitive market.[116] Several methods have been proposed for individuals to discover their innovative talents. In the case of employees, their creativity can be extinguished if the needed connection is not made by managers between them and their jobs.[117] Assigning jobs that suit recruits will help them to be challenged and prevent a situation in which they are endangered or overwhelmed.[118] Furthermore, the promotion of creativity at the workplace requires the right framework for it to thrive. A recommended method that can be applied is described as the T-shaped mind. Since creativity rests on the ability to merge existing dissimilar elements in new ways, the application of the T-shaped model will expand the understanding of individuals across multiple disciplines and expertise in various subjects.[119] Brainstorming is also used in formal sectors to generate ideas and develop talents. With the application of this technique quite a number of ideas are generated from each session. The basis of the use of the brainstorming method is that a group would generate many more ideas from different perspectives than an individual.[120]

The act of listening has been identified to awaken our inspiration, which is required to steer innovation. Individuals and businesses need to listen to the world if they desire to innovate. This action of listening involves having a broad mind without any planned agenda, while the focus of attention should be on details, facts, information and logical thinking. Data obtained from the process of listening have the capability and outstanding feature of revealing facts and hidden issues. Engaging in this activity thus requires individuals to reject nothing but pick up something even though it is different from what we know. In order to enhance our creativity there is need for the act of listening to be rehearsed for better concentration of our knowledge and interests. The outcome of the above will result in a push for competitive opportunities.[121] Besides the aforementioned, the survival of the fittest model can also be applied as another technique to kindle innovation.[122]

Essentially, the visualisation of information is considered an effective way of presenting information. Bearing this in mind, it is important to highlight the task of keeping records when creating ideas. The necessity of documenting, sketching and possible construction of models will give a better judgement of insights of ideas created. Moreover, valuable ideas have a tendency to be lost if they are not recorded.[123]

## Imbibing creativity

In the management of entrepreneurial innovation, there is a need to incorporate personal and environmental factors that influence behaviours.[124] The Complete solutions to problems are sometimes derived from innovative ideas prompted by many factors. At the same time, ideas from one field can be applied to an entirely new field.[125] Similarly, every innovation action now requires input from a range of diverse contributors.[126] In the light of the above, value creators should be convinced to extend their access to experts' experience and solutions in fields beyond their industries and conventional boundaries.[127] Put differently, learning opportunities can be potentially lost whenever knowledge is not dispersed.[128]

Customers on their part have an important role to play in innovation promotion even though their contributions are often underscored. They can originate and lead the modification process towards the production of appropriate products that align with their goals. Innovation led by consumers can be a fall out of the desire, or interest of a specific individual or group, upon the realisation of their dissatisfaction with available products and the action taken to address it.[129]

Overall, companies and individuals must view creativity as a performance enhancing channel. Beyond this, creativity is also required for quality and performance.[130] This chapter has emphasised that creative thinking is one of the methods through which creativity can be initiated. People attempt problems from the standpoint of their personality and conduct, using creative thinking.[131] On the other hand, responsive thinking entails knowledge acquisition in the framework of selective programmes that distinguish appropriate information. The way forward is to merge pieces of information in novel ways.[132]

## Notes

1  Pine (1991).
2  Baregheh, Rowley and Sambrook (2009).
3  Jay and Ria (1999).

4 McLaughlin and Caraballo (2013).
5 Jay and Ria (1999).
6 McLaughlin and Caraballo (2013).
7 Assink (2006).
8 Koellinger (2008).
9 Harless (1986).
10 Kiely (1993).
11 Jay and Ria (1999).
12 Richards (1998).
13 Nakamura and Mihaly (2002).
14 Meyer (2013).
15 Nakamura and Mihaly (2002).
16 Koellinger (2008).
17 Koellinger (2008).
18 Johansson (2004).
19 Huber, Kaufmann and Steinmann (2017).
20 Jay and Ria (1999).
21 Weiser (2011).
22 Coulson-Thomas (2017).
23 Kiely (1993).
24 Jay and Ria (1999).
25 Schonberger (1987).
26 Peters (1987).
27 Hamel and Prahalad (1994).
28 Jay and Ria (1999).
29 Koestler (1989).
30 Jay and Ria (1999).
31 Luoma-aho and Halonen (2010).
32 Lawson and Samson (2001).
33 Richards (1998).
34 Luoma-aho and Halonen (2010).
35 OECD (2010).
36 Meyer (2013).
37 Wang and Ahmed (2004).
38 McLaughlin and Caraballo (2013).
39 Huber, Kaufmann and Steinmann (2017).
40 Karlsson and Törlind (2013); Hansen and Andreasen (2006).
41 Huber, Kaufmann and Steinmann (2017).
42 Huber, Kaufmann and Steinmann (2017).
43 McLaughlin and Caraballo (2013).
44 Richards (1998).
45 Böhmer and Lindemann (2015).
46 Bakker, Boersma and Oreel (2006).
47 Karlsson and Törlind (2013).
48 Gillier, Kazakci and Piat (2012).
49 Koestler (1989)
50 Allen (1977).
51 Richards (1998).
52 McLaughlin and Caraballo (2013).
53 Basadur (2004).

54  Basadur (2004).
55  Kiely (1993).
56  Meyer (2013).
57  Urbancova (2013).
58  Urbancova (2013).
59  Martín-de Castro, Delgado-Verde, Navas-López and Cruz-González (2013).
60  Andreessen (2011).
61  Spender (1996).
62  Andreessen (2011).
63  Johansson (2004).
64  Adams (2005).
65  Meyer (2013).
66  Shapiro (2002).
67  Meyer (2013).
68  Weiser (2011).
69  Christensen, Ojomo and Van Bever (2017).
70  Meyer (2013).
71  Meyer (2013).
72  Meyer (2013).
73  Meyer (2013).
74  Meyer (2013).
75  Prahalad (1993).
76  Kandampully (2002).
77  Schumpeter (1939).
78  McLaughlin and Caraballo (2013).
79  Wef (2014).
80  Koellinger (2008).
81  Huber, Kaufmann and Steinmann (2017).
82  MacKenzi (1998).
83  Joe, Bessant and Pavitt (2005).
84  Adams (2005).
85  Richards (1998).
86  Assink (2006).
87  Koellinger (2008).
88  Adams (2005).
89  Assink (2006).
90  Meyer (2013).
91  Romero and Martínez-Román (2012).
92  Amabile (1998).
93  Bakker, Boersma and Oreel (2006).
94  Nakamura and Mihaly (2002).
95  Adams (2005).
96  Assink (2006).
97  Urbancova (2013).
98  Shapiro (2002).
99  Richards (1998).
100 Assink (2006).
101 Baiyere and Roos (2011).
102 Shapiro (2002).

103 Romero and Martínez-Román (2012).
104 Urbancova (2013).
105 Adams (2005).
106 Coulson-Thomas (2012).
107 Birchall and Tovstiga (2005)
108 Kogut and Zander (1992).
109 Prahalad (1993).
110 Amit and Schoemaker (1993); Grant (1991); Makadok (2001).
111 Assink (2006).
112 Adams (2005).
113 MacKenzi (1998).
114 Meyer (2013).
115 Assink (2006).
116 Luoma-aho and Halonen (2010).
117 Urbancova (2013).
118 Amabile (1998).
119 Adams (2005).
120 Adams (2005).
121 Adams (2005).
122 Meyer (2013).
123 Shapiro (2002).
124 Richards (1998).
125 Wang and Ahmed (2004).
126 Harrison and Waluszewski (2008); Perks and Moxey (2011).
127 Harrison and Waluszewski (2008); Perks and Moxey (2011).
128 Meyer (2013).
129 Kooskora (2004).
130 Hippel (2005).
131 Kiely (1993).
132 Adams (2005).

# 3   Overcoming barriers
to innovation

## Introduction

It has been widely accepted that businesses are responsible for inspiring the development of new ideas and the efficient use of their assets for economic growth and development.[1] Without a doubt, value creation is considered a strategic measure for the continued existence of firms,[2] particularly in the midst of drastic changes surrounding their operations. In reaction to the renewed business environment, there is need for firms to reevaluate their activities in line with their goal of satisfying customers.[3] Bearing in mind the importance of the above, innovation should be seen as an essential competence that organisations should possess.[4] It should not be considered only from the standpoint of a proficiency skill, rather it should be adopted as a way of life in the corporate world. Doing this will ensure that companies continually look to the future to determine and anticipate the significance of imminent value. This action will also spell out how they should determine the right blend of their offering, namely quality of product and services, and price.[5]

As a positive step, many companies are beginning to commit to innovation in response to the increased awareness of its need at all levels.[6] The significance of integrating innovation as part of a company's operations is to enable the firm, to compete effectively in the changing business environment by generating new products, services and processes. The next important step following the adoption of innovation by a firm is to sustain it. This process, it should be pointed out, is not an easy task to accomplish.[7] Facts about innovation development reveal that the process involves the exploration, growth and application stages. The cross-exchange of ideas at the various stages mentioned is fundamental for innovation to thrive.[8] It is not only new knowledge that is applicable for this process, but existing knowledge combined in creative ways can also bring about many innovations.[9]

There is a general consensus amongst experts that innovation begins with good ideas that should be converted into revenue-generating products, services and processes. For managers of firms, they resort internally to functional teams to ignite creativity, and with a good sense, can get a better understanding of what they have within.[10] The innovation process, as previously stated, starts with the ideation phase where a large number of ideas are generated and thereafter evaluated.[11] If the market introductions of the selected best ideas are successful, then the products are qualified as genuine innovations. Nevertheless, only a proportion of the innovative ideas assessed to have prospects eventually turn out to be successful.[12]

Generating tons of good ideas is one thing; the bottom-line however is how companies handle these ideas. New thoughts would not do well without strict screening and funding systems. They would rather create bottlenecks and problems across the organisation. In searching for ideas, companies should also consider external sources. Insights from customers, competitors (within and outside a firm's industry), and universities, etc. are viable sources of generating ideas and resources as well.[13]

## The importance of resources

In examining the competencies of firms, there is need to discuss the subject of assets. The resources of firms are regarded as their substantial possessions hence they should be made more effective. In recent years, the determination of the effective use of assets has been of concern to many.[14] A firm's resources are made up of physical and non-physical holdings. There are other types of assets that are described as intangible, which include a firm's capabilities, processes, information, technology and knowledge amongst others. The term under reference determines the capability of an enterprise to conceive and implement strategies.[15] Resourcing in innovation has to do with the internal lack of competence which has corresponding fundamental implications for a firms' innovative capacity.[16] Of the different resources possessed by firms, individuals are considered the most outstanding, and their value and contribution to the innovation process are evident. Given that one of the important roles of innovation is to satisfy the needs of customers, the first and important responsibility of firms therefore is to identify these needs. In as much as the needs in question here, originate from people, the human resource of firms hence have the responsibility of spotting out the needs.[17]

Bearing in mind the importance of a nation's resources, there is need to acknowledge that, with the advent and relevance of technology, the composition will continue to be redefined.[18] The resultant effect of this development is that resources considered to be valuable to-day may not remain the same in the future, especially when a better-quality alternative emerges.[19] Put differently, with the development of new knowledge, the value of resources can increase, or fade away. In consideration of the above, many resources considered valuable to-day will subsequently become irrelevant and worthless in the future.[20] When reclassifying the strength of a business therefore, already es-tablished practices sometimes become rigidities and challenges, since they are often implicit.[21] On the other hand, intense personal mental styles are usually not given up peacefully.[22] Another perspective of the above, stresses the fact that the distinctive relevant expertise of a firm today may become its core absurdity in the future, especially with the introduction of radical innovation.[23] Overall, with the turn of events in the business environment, the underlining focus of resources has shifted from the physical standpoint to knowledge base.[24]

## Barriers to innovation

The inevitable need for innovation in economic development, with the associated success of businesses in a fast transforming global world, has become a widely accepted notion.[25] We cannot con-structively discuss the unavoidable need for innovation in firms and nations without highlighting the limitations associated with its im-plementation. These challenges have brought about far-reaching dis-cussions on the subject.[26] The focus of this chapter is to put forward different approaches of overcoming the identified obstacles in order to benefit from engaging in innovation activities. Despite the already highlighted benefits of innovation, it should be pointed out that it is not a painless process. Sometimes it comes with risks and can be complicated to administer.[27] Although there are several documented achievements in the field of innovation, there are still proofs of many failed attempts,[28] thus confirming the possibility that the outcome of an innovation effort can fall short of the desired expectations.[29] Clearly, a number of innovative projects have been botched just be-fore being launched or unveiled in the market.[30] In reality, only a small fraction of evaluated ideas considered to have great prospects eventually flourish. The bulk of those that become successful are sometimes due to the willpower of the idea originator.[31] It is therefore not uncommon to see a number of viable innovation proposals aban-doned by one firm eventually get lost to their rivals.[32]

Again, previous business successes in the form of formulas are known to slow down the capacity of companies to 'unlearn'. Unlearning is depicted as the process by which people and firms do away with old logic and replace them with fundamentally new reasoning. The above action requires the examination of the validity of beliefs while assessing the current method of doing things.[33] Sadly, many small firms in the face of other challenges confronting them are deterred from adopting innovation because of the already-mentioned concerns.[34]

It is not unusual to see the foremost players in the market being trapped by their own success. Unsurprisingly, there are cases where newcomers from outside the industry of incumbents, successfully introduce pioneering technological breakthroughs and business models that disrupt the market. For example, the Enterprise software (ERP) was developed by SAP, and not by IBM or Microsoft. In another case, Nokia, the market leader at one time, was not the company that invented the mobile telephone with a camera, instead, Ericsson and Sony did. On the whole, the power composition of an organisation generally determines the rational model it will adopt.[35]

Despite the benefits of technology, it has not been readily adopted by some business organisations. This is because many large organisations do not possess the administrative capacity to take up and benefit from new technology. They are also not able to deal with the challenges that will enable them to take advantage of disruptive opportunities.[36] In considering the above, the lack of foresight can be regarded as a major obstacle to effective innovation.[37]

The introduction and the preceding paragraphs form the background for the discussion on innovation barriers which are factors that hinder firms from benefiting from innovation and related activities. Although there are several identified barriers that can limit the development of innovation, the important point to note is that these barriers can be overcome by specific actions and behaviours; therefore, they should not constrict the ability of individuals and companies to innovate.

The concept of pre-action barriers will be briefly discussed prior to highlighting the barriers to innovation. Some identified impediments to businesses are referred to as pre-action barriers. They are described as measures of companies taken when approaching issues such as avoiding reality by not taking decisions when results are not favourable, and when they realise they are in the wrong place. It further shows the inability of firms to lead transformational change, or create something new by destroying the old.[38] The example of the music industry gives us a vivid description of the above. Players in the industry held on to the mindset from the old order and paid dearly afterwards, for limiting the surge of the new online music business led by Apple's iTunes, Music Store and iPod.[39]

Generally, innovation barriers can be categorised as external and internal.[40] These categories can be further classified as supply, demand and environmental obstacles. Difficulties in acquiring technological information, raw materials and funds fall under the supply barrier category, while those related to customer needs and the risk of innovation are classified as demand barriers. Environmental innovation obstacles, on the other hand, include but are not limited to government regulations, policies and antitrust measures.[41] Yet, another type of barrier we can easily connect with is that described as market barrier. It is concerned with the dominance of markets by incumbents and the uncertainty in demand.[42] Meanwhile; the obstacles to market introduction are grouped into two. First, the projected price level can either be too high or low and second, the market introduction timing is regarded as too early or late.[43] Nonetheless, the inaction of the lower-level organisation and its bureaucracy, which are directly linked to the size of the firm, can undermine its innovative drive.[44]

The product development stage is another area where the effect of barrier to innovation is visible. At the early stage of the innovation process, prototypes of ideas generated are made. This activity requires time, commitment and investment in some cases. It takes a while sometimes, for generated ideas to be discussed and shared with others before it moves to the development stage. Besides time, the construction of a prototype may require some form of investment by the innovator. The enumerated process above can cause delays and eventually limit innovation.[45] The upshot of barriers on the innovative character of a firm or its achievement can be at different stages while the nature of its impact could be minor or significant. For instance, the non-availability of funds could have a major impact on the implementation phase of a product development.[46] Suffice to mention that rigid budgets, traditional thinking and firm funding criteria all combine to close down a good number of new ideas.[47]

Obstacles to forming disruptive innovations can also stem from the ineptness of firms to figure out the way things are done.[48] Another barrier to worthwhile disruptive innovation is the lack of courage of leaders of companies particularly in an environment that supports a management style of control rather than trust. Oftentimes, the necessary infrastructure is non-existent or underdeveloped, for disruptive innovation to be easily incorporated.[49] Other elements that can restrict our capacity to innovate include barriers centred on the competition for capital. Within a firm, divisions sometimes contend for inadequate funds to enable them meet their needs.[50] In the face of the above challenge, most times, there is limited capital available for the enterprise to meet their business needs. As a result, they would be favourably disposed to using available funds for secured investments rather than on innovations they consider risky.[51] Perhaps, this is responsible for the decline in research and development activities in some organisations.[52]

Generally, many firms are afraid to take the bold step towards innovation. This fear is deemed to be the motive behind their deliberate risk averse attitude which doubles as a barrier to innovation.[53] Given that undertaking risks may require a firm to cannibalise its successful product in the market, the resolution to take this daring decision of competing against its product rests specifically with management. Failure of management in this case in point, to take the right decision, can impede disruptive innovation.[54] Other Possible reasons why firms may be hesitant in the timely promotion of radical innovation with tendencies of competing with existing products[55] could be as a result of their current investments and assets. By the time they eventually decide and take action, it is sometimes too late.[56]

The self-effacing human resource knowledge base assumed by firms, more often than not, increases their incapability of carrying out a thorough evaluation of risks involved in actions and decisions to be taken.[57] Barriers that are specifically related to the management of an organisation are described as mindset barriers,[58] which is described as the inability to unlearn. The notion, 'to unlearn,' has been earlier defined, but because of its critical role, it is being reemphasised. This act is considered as one of the essential abilities required by individuals to surmount pre-judgement and outdated mental modes.[59]

## Overcoming innovation barriers

With the increase in technological innovation, it has become difficult for a single individual to denote in advance practical knowledge that will be relevant in the future.[60] Surely, breakthrough innovations are impressive achievements to realise; nevertheless, they are not easy to develop. Building them sometimes requires time, and could involve some risks, mostly in uncertain terms.[61] Expectedly, the high cost of innovation activities is also considered a restriction for firms. This is compounded by another barrier for businesses, described as having limited information on the availability of external support,[62] and closely related to the location of partners' constraint.[63] Undeniably, resources are directly linked to the long term sustainability and revenue generation of firms.[64] It is clear that being deficient in resources can contribute to personnel and capability limitations of an enterprise. On the whole the discovery of new solutions can be delayed by available capacity, while delays in time to innovate can also slow down the process.[65]

The above scenario is applicable to manufacturing firms as well. For them, the internal resources and cash-generating jobs contribute to their aggressive circles. Financial barriers have moreover been identified as harmful to their long-term sustainability and revenues.[66] From another standpoint, SMEs are more liable to face capability and resource restrictions than larger companies.[67]

At times, income expectations indirectly act as barriers for firms. Here, the high income anticipation and pressure to predict financial return on investment ultimately become barriers when projections are not met.[68] In the light of the above a company would perceive that its revenue would be threatened if it introduces technological change, thus creating a barrier that needs to be surmounted.[69] Meanwhile, aggressive revenue prospects and the goal of disruptive innovations can restrain managers from taking the right decision of choosing appropriate targets in emerging markets. What is more, the focus on financial projections can also lead to the non-inclusion of product features that will entice customers in existing markets where disruptive technologies will find their initial success, even though the products are being delivered expensively.[70]

Barriers related to personnel can be attributed to exhaustion factors individuals have.[71] Surely, the lack of technical experts,[72] together with the non-availability of standards in the area of design[73] can adversely affect a firm's performance in innovation development. In the same way, insufficient managerial knowledge and specialised skills are known to limit the ability of double-loop, meta-learning and unlearning.[74] Without doubt, the barriers mentioned, in one way or the other, limit innovation by individuals and firms with an overall effect on the development of innovation in countries within the African continent. Fortunately, for African nations, the pace of innovation can still be accelerated with the measures and actions put forward. Consideration and implementation of these measures can enable innovators to overcome several of the barriers listed. If this is achieved, the concerns and obstructions to business innovation in the continent would be addressed.[75]

One of the essential qualities required for overcoming barriers and promoting innovation is the skill of unlearning This skill will enable entrepreneurs replace traditional methods with essentially new ones.[76] Relatedly, using the barrier approach to promote innovation, supposes that the identification and understanding of the concept's obstacles and the application of successive actions in eradicating them will restore naturally its flow.[77] An alternative recommended approach that can be applied is to separate barriers between disciplines while at the same time combining knowledge of creative individuals in new ways. It is worthy to point out that shared knowledge and thinking processes are important for organisations. These firms are required to co-operate creatively with other companies by breaking and establishing new connections.[78] Being open to good ideas from beyond our confines and taking advantage of them are considered as viable techniques of overcoming barriers. For sure, valuable ideas can originate from a company's internal and external environments.[79]

On the whole, ideas tend to move easily through more adaptable entrepreneurial companies with less structured roles and authority, than in bureaucratic organisations.[80] Recognisably, successful innovations can also take place in spite of the environment of a company and the absence of the support of senior management. This can materialise when disruptive innovation projects are pursued by motivated project champions. The example of the emergence of the PlayStation idea within Sony illustrates the aforesaid point clearly.[81]

As already stated, the generation of good ideas is essential for innovation. It is however the responsibility companies to ensure that these ideas are not mishandled, given that new concepts would not prosper without strict selection and funding mechanism.[82] Surmounting capital constraints towards innovation development entails creating and fostering a system where capital can easily be accessed particularly by start-ups. This proposed measure will have a strong effect on African economies if they are implemented. Furthermore, an increase in patents will also be facilitated in an improved business environment with relevant infrastructure.[83] The constraint associated with the innovative character of firms can be overcome by the creation of a marketplace of ideas, although this may not completely resolve this challenge.[84] What is more, The rapid changes in the market have made it more difficult and at the same time essential for businesses to think in the light of the future.[85]

An appropriate example of how the barriers to innovation were reduced is the case of two Scandinavian countries. The Governments of Finland and Sweden realised that capital formation was a problem for the lucrative paper producing hardware business, and they intervened by giving substantial assistance. Funds were made available to the paper industry to enable the sale of software worldwide.[86] Consequently, for these forest products, Scandinavians now manage a well-harmonised cooperative programme between the stakeholders, namely paper industry, the machinery manufacturers and government.[87] The cooperative programme they operated, enabled them to overcome the barrier of inadequate capital.

Yet, another case of how innovation was used to address the challenge of existential need is the example of Israel which is known to have natural resources constraints. Despite these limitations, the barrier of inadequate agricultural land was addressed by the development of technology for growing agricultural products. Irrigation solutions, water treatment and desolation are innovative technologies that were applied to overcome the lack of water barrier.[88] In addition, in the absence of abundant energy resources, the sun has also been used widely by the country, to develop solar products and processes.[89] Some of the successful approaches used by Israel can be adopted and implemented by African nations. Rather than see available resources as impediments, the positive way to go is to work around our existential needs, with the assets we have.[90]

Indisputably, matching innovation with needs is another way to overcome barriers. Again, this approach was used by Israel in the area of security. The country developed advanced defence technology to overcome its security challenge in line with its goal of establishing a strong defence measure.[91] The support of government in overcoming barriers associated with innovation can take the form of tax credits and direct investments.[92] Enterprises can also be assisted with the allotment of additional financial resources particularly at the early phases of development.[93]

Taking a cue from the methods adopted by nations in overcoming the innovation barriers they faced, businesses in Africa will be transformed for sustained development in no distant future. The action of Swedish firms in reducing their innovation barriers gives insight into practical steps the country implemented to surmount the challenges they faced. In this case, politicians and other parties promptly reduced the gap between political public speaking and practical application, by crafting a tax system where small firms are treated fairly. Besides this, the employment laws were modified to significantly engage the rising population in creative training and entrepreneurship.[94] Furthermore, linking academic and research institutes has been identified as an alternative process that is expected to achieve results in the course of overcoming barriers.[95]

A different method that should be explored by firms is increasing intrinsic motivation. Doing this will boost the enthusiasm of individuals to collaborate and share information.[96] The unreserved and generous recognition of creative work even before the marketable impact of the outcome is necessary, while supervisory encouragement is also required to prevail over certain barriers.[97] A close cooperation within management, in addition to having practice and process driven structures, will also encourage innovation within the organisation.[98]

It is pertinent to state here that different stakeholders have a role to play in reducing innovation barriers. On the part of organisations, undertaking risks and accommodating failures would bring about more successful innovations. An organisational culture with a positive attitude towards risks is highly commendable. Once firms encouraged to take risks and tolerate failures, they are more likely to see successful innovations.[99]

## Conclusion

Certainly, Regional development agencies,[100] can play a role by supporting firms to overcome the identified obstacles they face. They can do this by establishing funds to cater for to the different phases of the innovation process such as building prototypes and carrying out investigation since these activities are usually under-supported. The provision of seed funds from these bodies[101] can also contribute to the seed capital required to enhance innovative ideas in institutions such as universities and laboratories.[102] Subsequent chapters of this book will look at other ways of building the innovation culture and sustaining growth.

Finally, it has been recognised that some nations are focused on the innovation mercantilism, which sometimes makes the concept thrive within their borders, but at the same time reduces innovation elsewhere. The global system in this circumstance is not designed in a way to encourage erring nations to do the right thing or dissuade others from taking the wrong step.[103] Africa is known for its abundant natural resources.[104] It is pertinent therefore for countries in the Continent to adopt new ways of utilising innovation for development, particularly in response to the rising costs of conventional growth models.[105] Without doubt, corporate innovation can be achieved with intangible qualities like flexibility.[106] With the integration of certain human activities and the development of research facilities in an inspiring environment, innovation will be promoted.

## Notes

1 Baas and Schrooten (2006).
2 Kotler and Keller (2008).
3 Doyle (2000).

 4  Hamel (2003).
 5  Tushman and Nadler (1986).
 6  Hamel (2003).
 7  Tushman and Nadler (1986).
 8  Teece, Pisano and Shuen (1997).
 9  Carlson and Wilmot (2006).
10  Hansen and Birkinshaw (2007).
11  Evershein (2003).
12  Huber, Kaufmann and Steinmann (2017).
13  Hansen and Birkinshaw (2007).
14  Andrews (1971).
15  Kandampully (2002).
16  Assink (2006).
17  McLaughlin and Caraballo (2013).
18  Kandampully (2002).
19  Kandampully (2002).
20  Kandampully (2002).
21  Meyer (2013).
22  Assink (2006).
23  Leonard-Barton (1992); Johannessen, Olsen and Lumpkin (2001).
24  Kandampully (2002).
25  Marques and Ferreira (2009); Porter (1996); Teece, Pisano and Shuen
    (1997); Zainol, Daud, Shamsu, Abubakar and Halim (2018).
26  Huber, Kaufmann and Steinmann (2017).
27  Chesbrough (2003a).
28  Huber, Kaufmann and Steinmann (2017).
29  Huber, Kaufmann and Steinmann (2017).
30  Vahs and Brem (2013).
31  Huber, Kaufmann and Steinmann (2017).
32  Huber, Kaufmann and Steinmann (2017).
33  Assink (2006).
34  Marques and Ferreira (2009).
35  Assink (2006).
36  Assink (2006).
37  Huber, Kaufmann and Steinmann (2017).
38  Baker and Sinkula (2002).
39  Assink (2006).
40  Piatier (1984).
41  Hansen and Birkinshaw (2007).
42  Assink (2006).
43  Assink (2006).
44  Eyal-Cohen (2019).
45  Hamel (2003).
46  Assink (2006).
47  Adams (2005).
48  Baker and Sinkula (2002).
49  Assink (2006).
50  Meyer (2013).
51  Meyer (2013).
52  Meyer (2013).

53  Meyer (2013).
54  Assink (2006).
55  Cravens, Piercy and Low (2002); Chandy and Tellis (1998).
56  Assink (2006).
57  Harel, Schwartz and Kaufmann (2019).
58  Assink (2006).
59  Assink (2006).
60  Tsoukas (1996).
61  Assink (2006).
62  Caputo, Cucchiella, Fratocchi, Pelagagge and Scacchia (2002).
63  Assink (2006).
64  Assink (2006).
65  Assink (2006).
66  Assink (2006).
67  Assink (2006).
68  Harper and Becker (2004).
69  Brown, J.S. (1998).
70  Assink (2006).
71  Lindsay, Perkins and Karanjikar (2009).
72  Xie, Zeng and Tam (2010).
73  Assink (2006).
74  Baker and Sinkula (2002).
75  Meyer (2013).
76  Baker and Sinkula (2002).
77  Assink (2006).
78  Adams (2005).
79  Hansen and Birkinshaw (2007).
80  Eyal-Cohen (2019).
81  Assink (2006).
82  Adams (2005).
83  Ojeaga (2015).
84  Hamel (2003).
85  Tushman and Nadler (1986).
86  Meyer (2013).
87  Meyer (2013).
88  Harel, Schwartz and Kaufmann (2019).
89  Harel, Schwartz and Kaufmann (2019).
90  Israeli Innovation Authority (2018); Breznitz (2007).
91  Harel, Schwartz and Kaufmann (2019).
92  Meyer (2013).
93  Assink (2006).
94  Myers and Assink (2006).
95  Meyer (2013).
96  Adams (2005).
97  Adams (2005).
98  Assink (2006).
99  Adams (2005).
100  Assink (2006).
101  Urbancova (2013).
102  Urbancova (2013).

103 Atkinson and Ezell (2013).
104 Christensen, Ojomo and Van Bever (2017).
105 Lee, Juma and Mathews (2014).
106 De Meyer, Nakane, Miller and Ferdows (1989).

# 4    Strategic partnerships

## Introduction

The environment of business today requires firms to connect with their customers and partners frequently. It also calls for the use of technology to offer services across local and international borders. The implementation of the above requires the utilisation of resources. As indicated in the preceding chapter, the resources of a firm include its capabilities, processes, information and knowledge which allows it to visualise and execute strategies.[1] Also, the crucial role of innovation in the sustenance of firms' competitive advantage and development has been established. Clearly, the increased interest in innovation management has brought about a positive influence on the development of the process.[2] Further discussion on practical steps to be taken for innovation to develop is therefore essential. The first point to highlight is the role of connection in the innovation system. Before discussing further, there is need to acknowledge the established connection between people, products and processes. Although these listed elements are required in innovation, without the involvement of individuals, innovation will not take place. Taking this into consideration, it implies that the interconnectivity and unification of the components of innovation should be emphasised.[3] Innovation is a fall out of what people do and it is increasingly being regarded as a consequence of business communication within and across boundaries. This concept of communication as indicated here can be between teams or operating units and is expressed in the interaction between a company, its partners and consumers.[4] There are practical examples to show that knowledge gained from other sources is harmonising. Applying this to firms, shows how acquired knowledge adds to what they already possess,[5] and increases the number of partners. This, in turn, will bring about enhanced prospects of acquiring valuable knowledge and maximize collaboration possibilities.[6]

Evidently, several innovations have emerged from the combination of existing knowledge in new ways.[7] On the other hand, a cross-exchange of ideas at the different phases of the innovation process, from exploration to application, is measured as an essential success factor.[8] Information dissemination and knowledge sharing are necessary at the early stage of the innovation process.[9] Not only is it required at this stage, it is also applicable at the marketing and adoption stages.[10] Increasingly, the expansion of innovation and distinctive abilities is reliant on non-tradable or non-codified knowledge.[11] The challenge however may be the sharing over distances, tacit or unstated knowledge.[12] Generally, knowledge develops from the interface between organisations and institutions and not necessarily from information accrued by a single establishment.[13] Furthermore, the requirements for innovation, discovery and invention are a combination of new and existing knowledge and information, while generated and learned knowledge should still be shared as part of the conditions of innovation development.[14]

## Networks, knowledge and innovation

With the upturn of events in the world, borderlines are no longer restricted and impermeable, rather they have become fluid, flexible and dynamic. In the face of the above, companies can now innovate using boundaryless cooperation, which entails encouraging groups, teams and networks with cross-functional businesses and capabilities, located in different areas, to connect.[15] Strikingly, the effect of the intrinsic characteristics of the innovation process portrays a geographical element that creates innovation clusters in certain locations.[16] Nokia is an example of a firm that benefited from the implementation and commitment to the boundaryless cooperative relationship. The company used this concept as part of its product and service upgrade process.[17]

Without a doubt, networks and networking as concepts, though not new in the area of science, are predominantly relevant today.[18] Business partners and customers can thereby engage in network organisations in order to co-create for their organic growth.[19] Membership of these networks can bring about a range of value even as affiliates have the opportunity to access intangible social assets embedded within the system.[20] Furthermore, the multiplicity of actors coming together will bring about an assortment of knowledge, competency, influence and authority amongst other factors.[21] On the other hand, it can lead to complications in innovation. Other elements such as variance in the goals of actors, technology and language can propel disagreement and ambiguity within the group.[22]

The network of activists has adopted an approach that is functional. It uses a bottom-up solution for development by creating solutions that react to local situations on top of useful interests of communities.[23] Another type of network that should be given attention is described as an extensive network. It is concerned with engaging actors that directly contribute to the innovation process,[24] as well as other participatory actors, for example, regulators and experts, who directly influence or impede the innovation procedures.[25] Similarly, socioeconomic networks[26] are recognised as important channels for increased learning.[27] They are made up of lasting webs of relationships among customers, suppliers and their related links to bodies like trade associations. These cross-organisational linkages help shape the building blocks of networks. They can be expressed as vertical, horizontal or lateral. While Vertical networks represent the interactions between firms at various stages of production, horizontal networks refer to connections between firms in the same industry producing similar products. On the other hand, lateral organisational connections are formed between production-wise unrelated firms. Additional details of the vertical network highlights the importance of overcoming innovation barriers in small or less developed countries particularly because of their links with foreign suppliers.[28]

The role of social networks is again exemplified by transition movement network models where local groups share their expertise and experiences amongst themselves. Learning is strengthened by the resources and standards obtained from media relations and consultancy. Here, the nature of the network is internal, as it supports its own development.[29] Furthermore, the social networks are recognised as carriers of ideas and practices that support the development of projects.[30]

Another important area that stands out is the connection between innovation and business ecosystems. Innovation should be considered as part of a business ecosystem an environment known to have a self-sustaining ability. As part of the business ecosystem companies require customers and resources to exist and innovation is considered as the central element of the system because it connects players within the system and flows back and forth between customers and companies.[31]

Within the business innovation ecosystem, customers play an important role from two perspectives. First, they drive innovation in organisations, and secondly they steer innovation externally by their influence on businesses and communities worldwide.[32]

Since internal innovations are habitually driven by the needs of customers[33] in the case of SMEs, consumers and suppliers have a part to play in the innovation process.[34] For innovation to turn out well, it should be pointed out that trust is required at the interpersonal and institutional levels.[35] The relevance of trust becomes more relevant because of the fundamental challenge companies face in establishing close relationships.[36] Incontestably, innovative activities have an impact on the overall rate of innovation, which is regarded as a function of the number of people connected and exchanging ideas.[37] In general, the overriding benefit of being part of a network is that it enables members to have access to affordable resources, expertise and advice.[38] As a final point, network partners also facilitate the concurrent adoption of knowledge from a variety of sources.[39]

## Innovation at the grassroots

Another area where innovation occurs and value is created, though sometimes overlooked, is the grassroots. Innovation at the grassroots illustrates how new bottom to top solutions in response to local situations are generated by activities of a network of neighbours, community groups and activists working with people. It also comes with varied activities of clusters and activists being organised for sustainable development. The power of the innovation system and the outcome lies with the grassroots communities.[40] Promoters of the grassroots initiative undertake experiments with social innovations and green technologies with other methods. It is worthy to mention that a number of these initiatives are available in the area of community food projects, co-housing and furniture recycling schemes.[41]

One reputable grassroots initiative that has encouraged the mobilisation of ideas, innovations and traditional practices is the Honey Bee Network in India. This organisation set off at first in search of developing innovations at the grassroots and thereafter started assisting in making these innovations readily available for use by members of the local communities towards the improvement of their lives. The innovative ideas and practices from across hundreds of districts in India are assembled together by volunteers making connections people in the communities.[42] The operation of the network concept under reference is weighed against the need for cross-pollination of ideas and learning in local dialects where applicable. Clearly, knowledge is shared here with the consent of the discoverer while the intellectual property rights of members are protected.[43]

As part of the operations of the Honey Bee Network, it does not limit itself to technological innovations alone. Communities also take charge of their resources by developing innovative rules to manage their natural resources. Teachers also have a part to play in this system by endorsing innovation in the educational scheme. Taking a cue from the above, African communities can effectively promote innovation.[44]

## Sustaining competitive advantage through strategic alliances

There are several traditional knowledge practices in Africa that can also be organised, modified and turned into useful products and processes that will create value for consumers. Clearly, managing the abundant natural resources of Africa towards innovation promotion can be achieved by adopting worthy initiatives like the Honey Bee Network model at the grassroots.[45] Apart from grassroots innovations, strategic alliances can also help promote innovation. These coalitions are principally applicable in product innovation, particularly in industries where changing technology is the order of the day.[46]

Alliances can enhance a firm's performance and innovation endeavours by granting access to new knowledge.[47] They are also recognised to avert obstacles and stimulate the process of innovation.[48] By means of horizontal and vertical strategic alliances with other companies and individuals, firms can resort to resourceful ways of developing products and services required by their customers even outside their domain and area of core competence.[49] With increased global competition, it is in the interest of firms to infiltrate leading clusters across the world with the objective of accessing new knowledge, especially in reaction to the pressure of increasing technological assets and innovation.[50] The emphasis is on co-operations beyond boundaries by creating a set of connections while the relationships built should be nurtured across the borders of the organisation.[51]

By attaching to a cluster, companies can obtain new components and equipment in addition to other relevant elements required to make the innovation process uncomplicated. Local suppliers and partners located within clusters on their part, can through analogous relationships get involved in the process of innovation.[52] It is important to state here that the effect of some productivity characteristics on innovation is substantial[53] while the innovation capacities of firms can instantly result in increased productivity. Overall, clusters are known for their role in revitalising the innovative capacities of enterprises.[54]

The benefits of innovation are underlined by the competitive environment of clusters and the drive for relentless improvement of existing technological resources.[55] Clusters are a viable means of encouraging the generation of new businesses,[56] essentially because the activities of start-ups are more prevalent in clusters than in remote locations. Connections and interactions among members in clusters and the information they share can propel prospects to discover business potentials they ordinarily would not have seen or considered.[57] The role of competition and collaboration in clusters is apparent and should therefore be supported[58] because of the immense benefits overtime, these elements will help members improve their product and service development activities.[59] Apart from the above, there are considerable advantages and prospects in innovation carried out by a group of people with different perspectives of a situation, even though this is not always straightforward and easy.[60]

Noticeably, the value of collaboration and the effectiveness of communication can be influenced by factors such as differences in knowledge and standards. Cultural goals have also been recognised to affect the flow of communication. For innovation to be deliberately implemented, there is need to adopt creative methods of building exchanges and synergy.[61] The illustrated role of clusters in the biotechnology industry is evident. Here, players are known to connect with other laboratories because the flow of knowledge is too complex for a single company to handle.[62] By and large, innovation will thrive where intangibles like social networks and trust abound.[63] In the pursuit of innovation therefore, current technological advancement has brought about deliberate interconnected networks for product development, assembling and distribution.[64] The advantages of these partnerships, therefore, should necessitate collaborations amongst locals and companies, to develop innovative products and services to solve common problems confronting them.[65]

In the light of the above, individuals, small and average sized firms, can actively participate in knowledge and technology creation while large organisations can search for ways to work in partnership with the knowledge architect.[66] It should be recognised that working collectively with formal structures like companies will direct the centre of attention to the path of addressing local needs.[67] As highlighted, for innovation to thrive at the organic level, it requires the combination of people, processes and products.[68] At the same time, diversity should be considered and included in productivity advancement opportunities that impact on innovation.[69]

Given that firms do not innovate single-handedly, their relationship with customers, suppliers, service providers, private and public organisations and rivals ought to contribute to their innovative activities. Therefore, the role of interactions in the innovation of firms when taken into consideration should be heightened.[70] Consequently, firms should be focused on customers and have a close connection with some of the earlier listed groups in addition to being more open to improved ways of doing things for the advantage of their clients. The application of effective methods in realising customers' needs can be achieved by firms, using technology, knowledge and networks. These elements stand out as a distinct set of factors capable of promoting innovation, especially when they are applied in service organisations. A combination of networks, knowledge and technology will also ensure that the focus of companies is on the utilisation of their assets towards the fulfilment of the unrevealed needs of customers.[71]

It should be emphasised that innovation development should not be the lone reason for a firm's collaborative activity. There are other grounds that should propel companies to interact and collaborate with others. Reducing the cost of technological development, minimising the risk element of market entry barriers in addition to achieving economies of scale, are other benefits firms can enjoy when they collaborate with others.[72] Without a doubt, the benefits of setting up and maintaining networks are enormous.[73] With regards to the structure and size of networks, it should be made clear that there is no optimal structure to be built, neither is there an approved number of connections that networks are mandated to have.[74] Apart from the issue of dimension, it is clear that the optimal strength and performance of networks does not depend on time and location.[75] Even though there is an established link between the created connections and the worth of ideas generated.[76]

There have been interesting results in the area of product development and distribution linked to organised networks across nations. These results have played a part in ensuring technological improvement in innovation contests.[77] Besides networks, regulated strategies are also key to the success of innovation.[78] Increasingly, customers are looking forward to be delighted by firms' creativity. For this reason, continuous creative innovation concepts should be implemented by enterprises on behalf of their customers.

This notion of continuous creative innovation is not only applicable to products related offerings but also relevant in service innovation which is typified by the growing expectations of customers.[79] Sustaining strong relationships with customers has thus become a fundamental strategy for service firms in all industries to adopt.[80] Another method of evaluating the competence of a firm is the area of its relationship with other groups. Developing and nurturing an enduring relationship with external and internal parties from the perspective of customers is judged as a fundamental proficiency of a firm.[81] The implementation of creative strategies will ensure that firms satisfy the ever-changing needs of customers. Beyond customers, the successful application of these strategies is for the ultimate benefit of the firm.[82]

As part of support for the course of innovation, a country can engage in cross-cutting factors where human and financial assets will be dedicated to scientific and technological progress.[83] There are also appropriate designed programmes that can train and guide personnel to focus on refined local customers. The earlier mentioned options earlier are viable strategies that can motivate a firm to dedicate its time and resources to establish relationships with bodies such as universities.[84]

In order to better understand how the development of innovation can be achieved in Africa, the concept of innovation infrastructure comes to bear. This structure specifies the effect of public policy on activities related to innovation and the level of technological complexities. Some well thought out policies include the protection of intellectual property, innovation tax-based incentives in addition to anti-trust enforcement and its consequence in promoting an open and competitive economy.[85]

Undoubtedly, the successful promotion and delivery of productive innovation rely on associations and networks operated by government-owned and private institutions. Having therefore a variety of end-user consortiums at the national, regional and divisional levels is judged as a contributing factor in innovation promotion.[86] Today, service organisations are compelled by the realities of global competition to transcend traditional boundaries and work in coalition with individuals and suppliers. In an effort to expand their core proficiency, they are required to search for professional and expert knowledge.[87] Surely, the competitive position of firms will improve significantly if they continuously expand their innovation network globally and plug into relevant clusters.[88]

## Engaging in networks

For Africa, there is need for countries within the continent to increase their commitment and focus on learning, in agreement with the needs of users while the centre of attention of national capacity building and policy formation should be based on institutions, with emphasis on innovation results.[89] Expounding further on the benefit of networks is the example of Danone, a dairy company specialised in the production of yogurt. The company developed in 2006 an improved nutritious product variant from its standard product. Danone worked in collaboration with the Government of Bangladesh to deliver a cheaper version of this new product as a strategy targeted at addressing the malnutrition problem the country was confronted with. This collaboration between the firm and the government of a country stimulated the creation of another product the company later developed that became successful in the market.[90]

An innovation network without any collaborators restrictions, can have united developers or members who relate freely. For instance, the university – industry – government collaboration with the purpose of enabling innovation in society is a good description that fits the described network.[91] Another type of partnership required for the growth of resources and technology is the Research and Development (R & D) network.[92] In order to support the integration of resources, deliberate actions are required by these coalitions.[93] Undeniably, the need for improved efforts in building an innovative nation is pertinent. This can be achieved through the promotion and growth of major technological innovations which will simultaneously improve entrepreneurship in general.[94]

There have been increased concerns over the years for the incorporation of customers as co-creators in promoting innovation development and creation of value.[95] In the course of time, the quality of relationships and interactions will determine the discovery of new sources of competitive advantage for firms. These relationships will further stimulate co-creating experiences between the companies and customers.[96] Above and beyond the already highlighted effect of collaboration between firms and customers, are intangible benefits such as customer loyalty and satisfaction that can be derived from the close ties they share.[97] For instance, in the food and drink industry, customers' involvement have been recognised to wield a significant impact. In this industry, the impact of innovation is limited, as majority of new introductions are concentrated within the range of extensions and new flavours.[98]

The need for networks in innovation development has extensively been outlined in this chapter. The important question that follows is how these networks can be formed for the benefit of participating members?. There are two different methods of building external networks.

The first approach involves the development of a solution aimed at finding answers to specific problems, while the second method is building a network with the aim of seeking new ideas within a broad technology or product area. The former approach has been adopted and built by A.G. Lafley at P & G, where internal product developers interpret customers' needs into technology briefs that contain descriptions of the problem to be solved. These briefs are then dispersed to the company's outer network, which is made up of a connection of technology scouts, research labs, suppliers and retailers across the world to see if someone out there can proffer solutions to the advertised problem.[99]

The application of the second method of setting up a network to spawn new ideas within a technology area is demonstrated in the strategy of the German-based electronics engineering company, Siemens, in Silicon Valley. The company assigned a number of professional representatives based in Berkeley, California, with the responsibility of connecting with scientists, doctoral students, entrepreneurs and researchers in government agencies and other centres.[100] On the other hand, a complementary approach to establishing an internal network is to make use of in-house cross units to generate new ideas from external sources. Networks formed in organisations using above method have fostered deliberations and exchanged knowledge amongst individuals in different sections.[101]

The underlying point in managing networks is diversity. This notion is pertinent and considered over and above the number of contacts in the network. The multiplicity and composition of a network group is an opportunity for members to access quite a number of unique sources of information and ideas.[102] In addition to the above, a far-reaching network of partners will further raise the chances of obtaining vital knowledge from members of the network.[103] More specifically, the partner-based innovation strategy enables partners to access each other's operational resources such as distribution channels and customer base. This technique if adopted by small firms will work in their favour by giving them access to valuable resources of large companies and subsequently help them overcome their liability of age and size. Large incumbent firms in return can access the technology of start-ups as well and make use of their external knowledge and expertise.[104]

In search of an appropriate innovation strategy, the concentration of firms should be on value. As long as companies focus on securing value for their customers, they can be sure of surpassing their competitors.[105] It has equally become important to motivate individuals and groups to connect within and outside their organisations for the promotion and acquisition of knowledge without any converse effect on the network.[106] Generally, the outcome of network interactions is a win-win situation for parties involved and the group as a whole, while concerted effort is usually geared towards solving problems.[107]

The outcome of the design of an innovation system, to a large extent, depends on certain cultural, economic and political factors, with great implications for national policy. The need for the creation of appropriate national institutions in our environment, for innovation to prosper, cannot be overlooked.[108] From the perspective of the benefits of innovation, it should be calculated as a strategic natural initiative required for the success of a company rather than a mere project. The moment innovation is regarded as a project, the necessary attention required from management will not be significant while the accompanying benefits to be derived will also be limited. It is therefore recommended that innovation should be regarded as a natural phenomenon for the success of businesses, just as people, processes, products and customers are tagged as essentials.[109]

Visibly, there is a distinction between networks established to administer inter-organisational connections and those formed to tap into external technology resources. The former are set up for the successful commercialisation of firms' innovations.[110] As a result of the rising number of networks, there has been a corresponding call in the market for cooperation within networks, particularly the multi-divisional ones, who are focused on technological innovations.[111] Network cooperation can also involve working teams comprising of public and private actors with clear divergent views.[112] A good example of the effect of having a good relationship between players in a network can be seen in the case of Caterpillar Peoria and its dealers. The network the company was affiliated with, resulted in the provision of better-quality service.[113]

There are other reasons put forward for the decision of companies to form affiliations. Sometimes, the determination to provide enhanced services for customers, propel companies to form partnerships. The decision of Air Canada to form an alliance with other partners illustrates this point. The Star Alliance partnership formed, amongst other things, provided flexibility for customers and a single interface for their comfort and benefit.[114] Partners, including rivals of Air Canada, also gained from the service advantage component of the partnership.[115] Ultimately, the result of developing non-imitable attributes is the accomplishment of the competitive advantage goals of companies.[116]

There are other prospective partners like universities and agencies of government that companies can readily connect and work with, to bridge the gap of their innovation pursuit. Since the above mentioned partners routinely conduct extensive studies and discoveries, they have viable contributions to make to the system.[117] These institutions also stand out from private actors because of their lack of profit objective, and involvement in continuous research not necessarily focused on the outcome not limited to time. Not necessarily focused on the outcome nor limited to time.[118] However, there is a different kind of connection formed for knowledge exchange that is important for organisational innovation. This alliance is referred to as communities of practices,[119] and it enables the sharing of knowledge, skills and information freely as a resource problem-solving approach.[120]

## Building partnerships for innovation development

By the adoption of partnering strategies, the possibility of lessening the risks associated with innovation can be achieved. Reducing risks has the potential of stimulating creativity and upgrading the quality of a company's innovative activities. Besides risk reduction issues, partnerships as part of their set up, allow for costs to be shared.[121] They can also lead to increased access to developed technology in different locations,[122] which, in turn, can bring about improved capabilities of harnessing the returns of innovation.[123]

The point to take from the discussion in this chapter is that there are a number of new themes that are now applicable in the pursuit of a company's strategy. Knowledge, foresight, proficiency and partnerships are considered as appropriate themes. Further related concepts include alliances, networks, ecosystems, transformation and renewals.[124] One of the advantages of implementing the above mentioned concepts is getting advice that will guide newly set up companies. These newly formed companies, with the help of established firms, can be linked with investors that can help them grow.[125]

Generally speaking, innovation and technological progress have been identified as the outcome of several interactions within a system.[126] At the grassroots level, apposite schemes, technologies and successful programmes as well as prototypes from other locations can be adapted and implemented to address peculiar needs. For instance, the concept of Hackerspaces and Makerspaces are springing up across many towns worldwide. Inspired by ideas from free software, open design and peer production, the above mentioned concepts are networked with one another, to form part of a global phenomenon that shares designs, instructions and codes over social media platforms. With this method, joint projects can be pursued and replicated internationally.[127] Furthermore, these networks make available to neighbours and local communities, resources such as small-scale industrial prototype technologies like laser cutters, micro-electronic controllers, design software and 3D printing amongst others. In addition, access to the use of other conventional hand tools, including lathes, drills and sewing machines are also available.[128]

Usually, Hackerspaces and Makerspaces are designed, like a maker's mindset, for creating something out of nothing and exploring interests. Acquired skills from the provided spaces are also useful in preparing those who require it for subjects such as science, engineering and mathematics. On the whole, the above mentioned spaces provide a communal place for learning and sharing where peer production practices can be applied on personal projects.[129]

In the quest for innovation advancement, grassroots innovation should be expanded with a number of techniques made available. For this reason, workshops, land, classrooms, laboratories, streets, office tools should be easily accessible at the grassroots. In the area of communication, various means of sharing, documenting and exchanging experiences can be explored in promoting innovation in the communities. While executing the above, innovation challenges and achievements can be a valuable source of information and experience.[130]

It is necessary at this point to introduce the important notion of *Innovation democracy*. This is one concept that deserves attention because it can uphold innovation in Africa if implemented. It is described as the capacity of people to challenge the path of innovation for every community to be reached, get involved and be empowered.[131] The contribution of grassroots innovation to democracy can be aided by redirecting the way society invests in innovation and considering fresh ways of supporting a number of innovative activities. Programmes that have been used effectively by many groups at the grassroots include prospects like crowdfunding which is used to access finance from external sources for immediate communities towards the implementation of viable initiatives.[132] Other practices used in promoting innovation right now are grassroots initiatives practices such as social technologies, open hardware, participatory design, agro-ecology, shared machine shops and others derived from the communities themselves.[133]

Open innovation, already discussed in earlier chapters, plays a role in fostering collaboration, therefore it should be given due consideration. With attention to organisational research using links and ecosystems, the effort of partners across networks is emphasised. Partners can come from an array of suppliers of raw materials and machinery as well as consumers of products.[134] Again, the transmission of knowledge across local and international institutions can be reinforced or deterred by certain factors[135] which can restrict a company's ability to benefit from business opportunities in established inter-organisational networks.[136] Similarly, the exchange of technology and knowledge between people, enterprises and institutions is recognised as a major determinant of the outcome of the innovation process.[137] Research institutes and universities are also known in the system, while their performance have significantly affected the general national innovation system.[138] Exploring the relationship between the listed institutions and innovation shows how securing property rights, having an effective judicial system and market-oriented policies, will work together at improving the rate of innovation.[139]

In the advancement of innovation, regional networks can also be used as a means of boosting the process. These networks share some similarities with clusters which have been earlier described as networks of institutional infrastructural frameworks that support innovation within a region.[140] The emphasis on geographical attention inspires team-like relationships and communication between actors involved in the innovation process. Regional networks further create a favourable environment for innovation within the region to make up in situations where members outside the region are not able to give their support.[141] Another advantage of a functional regional culture is the promotion and circulation of implicit knowledge that creates a unique environment for continuous innovation stimulation.[142]

## Conclusion

With the integration of the world economy, several opportunities that firms can take advantage of, have been uncovered, while competencies and capabilities can be leveraged from the renewed environment.[143] Prior to this time, activities of firms were limited to their home country or region. The location limitation of businesses and their strategy has however been improved upon, with development in communication, transportation and other related systems.[144] Consequently, the new trade and industry reality has extended the value chain of firms across locations[145] while the advantages of innovation partnering have been highlighted. Inspite of these benefits, there are some shortcomings associated with operating partnerships. Some of the weaknesses of the system include managing and protecting intellectual property rights in the partnership relationship. Also, the active engagement of many partners may bring about relationship management and monitoring challenges,[146] with the related weakness of complexity in absorbing knowledge from different sources.[147]

Since innovation does not take place in seclusion, it has been established that networks are essential in improving the capacity of innovation and its response to the needs of users. These networks can be made up of public and private agents like public institutions such as universities and government-owned establishments together with other groups of end users.[148] The importance of highlighting the role of these institutions and their impediments in the innovation process is because, at the initial stage of market innovation, formal and informal institutions are necessary.[149] For public sector agents however, the innovation process starts with the search for primary building blocks of technology.[150] Once these building blocks are established by the public agents, private entities like companies can then work to get them licensed and obtain patents for those they are interested in using.[151] Public institutions are further known to stimulate the pervasion of internal research laboratories while public agents like universities, because of their non-profit nature, can sustain huge economic losses incurred in research.[152] If a new product ultimately emerges from the activities they are engaged in, part of the accrued economic gains will be distributed between the private and public sector agents.[153]

In sum, the nature of an institution's environment, to a large extent, affects its growth. By implication, a constructive institutional environment blossoms while a hostile one diminishes. With a favourable system in place, a nation's economy can be developed and sustained.[154] There is need to highlight the concept of internal cross-unit network which stands out as a complementary method of generating new ideas within a company's external environment. The supposition here is that individuals who are not familiar with each other can work together to generate ideas on request. What is essential for this activity to take place is the establishment of an unending channel of communication and exchange of knowledge between members of different teams.[155]

Besides institutions, there are available incubators that can also aid businesses seeking growth. Some of them are dedicated to helping existing businesses achieve their goals by offering financial and business supports.[156] Undoubtedly, innovation partnership as a novel event has influenced many industries today. Although there are several cases where firms were unable to strengthen their innovative efforts as a result of problems they encountered in the environment, the solution of resorting to collaborative networks for increased performance possibilities via learning from partners, users, customers and suppliers is an appropriate strategy to adopt.[157]

## Notes

1 Kandampully (2002).
2 Kaplan and Norton (2004); Hamel andPrahalad (1994); Rothwell (1994); Van de Ven, Polley, Garud and Venkataraman (1999); Van der Panne, Van Beers and Kleinknecht (2003); Verloop (2004); Cooper (2005); Lazonick (2005); Pavitt (2005); Powell and Grodal (2005); Tidd and Bessant (2009).
3 McLaughlin and Caraballo (2013).
4 Gratton (2006).
5 Roper, Dub and Love (2008).
6 Roper and Xia (2014).
7 Carlson and Wilmot (2006).
8 Estrin (2009).
9 Estrin (2009).
10 Luoma-aho and Halonen (2010).
11 Maskell and Malmberg (1999); Asheim and Gertler (2005).
12 Haldin-Herrgard (2000); Howells (2002); Asheim and Gertler (2005).
13 Kalua, Awotedu, Kamwanja and Saka (2009).
14 Howells (2002).
15 Gratton (2006).
16 Haldin-Herrgard (2000); Howells (2002); Asheim and Gertler (2005).
17 Gratton (2006).
18 Estrin (2009).
19 Coulson-Thomas (2017).
20 Varis and Littunen (2010).
21 Corsaro, Cantù and Tunisini (2012); Öberg and Shih (2014).
22 Aarikka-Stenroos and Sandberg (2012); Corsaro, Cantù and Tunisini (2012); Corsaro, Ramos, Henneberg and Naudé (2012).
23 Seyfang and Haxeltine (2012).
24 Perks and Moxey (2011).
25 Meyer (2013).
26 Granovetter (1985).
27 Meyer (2013).
28 Assink (2006).
29 Hopkins and Lipman (2009).
30 Geels and Raven (2006).
31 McLaughlin and Caraballo (2013).
32 McLaughlin and Caraballo (2013).
33 McLaughlin and Caraballo (2013).
34 Doloreux (2004); Rhee, Park and Lee (2010).
35 Ellonen, Blomqvist and Puumalainen (2008).
36 Gratton (2006).
37 Chesbrough (2003a). Chesbrough (2003b)
38 Andreessen (2011).
39 Gupta, Sinha, Koradia, Patel, Parmar, Rohit, Patel, Patel, Chand, James, Chandan, Patel, Prakash and Vivehanandan (2003).
40 Seyfang and Smith (2007).

41 Church and Elster (2002).
42 Gupta (2013).
43 Gupta (2013).
44 Gupta (2013).
45 Kandampully (2002).
46 Visnjic, Wiengarten and Neely (2016).
47 Inkpen (1996).
48 Feldman (1994); Porter (2000); Fagerberg (2005).
49 Peppers and Rogers (1997).
50 Tinguely (2013).
51 Torrance (1972).
52 Porter and Stern (2001).
53 Porter (1998); De Beule, Van Den Bulcke and Zhang (2008). Simmie (2008).
54 Porter (1998).
55 Breschi, Lissoni and Montobbio (2005); Cumbers, MacKinnon and Chapman (2008).
56 Porter (1998); Breschi (2008) Isaksen (2008).
57 Porter (1998); Scott (2006); Fingleton, Igliori and Moore (2008); Delgado, Porter and Stern (2010).
58 Porter (1998); Audretsch, Lehmann and Warning (2005); Feldman (2008); Rees (2005).
59 Polenske (2004).
60 Barlow (2007).
61 Barlow (2007).
62 Chesbrough (2003a).
63 Moenaert, Caeldries, Lievens and Wauters (2000).
64 Weiser (2011).
65 Daniels (2014).
66 Chesbrough (2003a).
67 Kraemer-Mbula and Wamae (2010).
68 McLaughlin and Caraballo (2013).
69 Tinguely (2013).
70 Fagerberg (2005).
71 Kandampully (2002).
72 Tidd, Bessant and Pavitt (2002).
73 Alm and McKelvey (2000).
74 Gemünden and Heydebreck (1995); Håkansson and Snehota (1989).
75 Varis and Littunen (2010).
76 Björk and Magnusson (2009).
77 Weiser (2011).
78 Huber, Kaufmann and Steinmann (2017).
79 Kandampully (2002).
80 Kandampully (2002).
81 Kandampully (2002).
82 Kandampully (2002).
83 Porter and Stern (2001).
84 Porter and Stern (2001).
85 Porter and Stern (2001).
86 Kalua, Awotedu, Kamwanja and Saka (2009).
87 Kandampully (2002).
88 Tinguely (2013).

89   Kalua, Awotedu, Kamwanja and Saka (2009).
90   Eyal-Cohen (2019).
91   Powell, Koput and Smith-Doerr (1996).
92   Perks and Moxey (2011); Rampersad, Quester and Troshani (2010).
93   Aarikka-Stenroos, Jaakkola, Harrison and Mäkitalo-Keinonen (2017).
94   Qui, Han and Jiang (2016).
95   VonHippel (2005); Tseng and Piller (2003); Von Hippel (2005).
96   Prahalad and Ramaswamy (2004).
97   Hansen and Birkinshaw (2007).
98   Galizzi and Venturini (1996); Grunert, Harmsen, Meulenberg, Kuiper, Ottowitz, Declerck, Traill and Goransson (1997).
99   Hansen and Birkinshaw (2007).
100  Hansen and Birkinshaw (2007).
101  Hansen and Birkinshaw (2007).
102  Hansen and Birkinshaw (2007).
103  Leiponen and Helfat (2010).
104  Powell and Brantley (1992); Gassmann and Keupp (2007).
105  Kim and Mauborgne (2005).
106  Björk and Magnusson (2009).
107  Meyer (2013).
108  Kalua, Awotedu, Kamwanja and Saka (2009).
109  McLaughlin and Caraballo (2013).
110  Vanhaverbeke and Cloodt (2006).
111  Biemans (1991); Håkansson and Waluszewski (2007); Powell, Koput and Smith-Doerr (1996); Rampersad, Quester and Troshani (2010).
112  Nissen, Evald and Clarke (2014); Reypens, Lievens and Blazevic (2016). Öberg and Shih (2014).
113  Jay and Ria (1999).
114  Baumol (2010).
115  Kalua, Awotedu, Kamwanja and Saka (2009).
116  Jay and Ria (1999).
117  Baumol (2010).
118  Bayh and Allen (2012).
119  Brown and Duguid (1991).
120  Wenger and Snyder (2000).
121  Powell (1998).
122  Niosi (2003).
123  Gemser and Wijnberg (1995).
124  Richards (1998).
125  Eyal-Cohen (2019).
126  Tinguely (2013).
127  Smith and Stirling (2016).
128  Smith, Hielscher, Dickel, Söderberg and van Oost (2013); Kohtala (2016).
129  Smith and Stirling (2016).
130  Smith and Stirling (2016).
131  Smith and Stirling (2016).
132  Smith and Stirling (2016).
133  Smith and Stirling (2016).
134  Dillon, Lee and Matheson (2005).
135  Malik (2013).

136 Vanhaverbeke and Cloodt (2006).
137 Kirner, SpomenkaMaloca, Rogowski, Slama, Oliver Som, Spitzley and Wagner (2007).
138 Ander (2006).
139 Guan and Chen (2012).
140 Mahagaonkar (2008).
141 Asheim and Gertler (2005).
142 Cooke (2001); Asheim and Gertler (2005).
143 Asheim and Gertler (2005); Cooke (2005); Edquist and Hommen (1999).
144 Dunning (1998); Dunning (2008); Ketels (2008).
145 Dunning and Lundan (2008).
146 Hertner and Jones (1986); Moore and Lewis (1999).
147 Simon (1947) Audretsch and Stephan (1996); Sieg, Wallin and Von Krogh (2010).
148 Roper and Xia (2014).
149 Kalua, Awotedu, Kamwanja and Saka (2009).
150 Oluwatobi, Efobi, Olurinola and Alege (2015).
151 Basadur (2004).
152 Mahagaonkar (2008).
153 Guan and Chen (2012).
154 Asheim and Gertler (2005).
155 Oluwatobi, Efobi, Olurinola and Alege (2015).
156 Hansen and Birkinshaw (2007).
157 Andreessen (2011).

# 5   Promoting innovation in our environment

## Adopting transformational innovation

The hallmark of the 21st century, to a large extent, is dependent on knowledge, information and an economy characterised by innovation.[1] With market globalisation, firms are now open to international competitive forces that will compel them to adapt in order to survive, particularly as the world is increasingly becoming more interrelated.[2] The effect of market globalisation is not peculiar to large firms. Small sized firms are equally affected and confronted with the documented challenges.[3] Innovation has been duly identified as one of the practical strategies for the continued existence and competitiveness of firms.[4] In response, businesses need to launch novel high-quality products and take advantage of new technology.[5] Successful innovation is not a trouble-free mission to accomplish, especially for enterprises with little experience and limited resources.[6] Clearly with the creation of new markets, there are enormous opportunities in the area of nonconsumption, therefore firms' risks should be internalised for the development of strong and sustaining enterprises.[7] Taking into consideration the above, every enterprise or corporation that desires to maintain its market position should innovate.[8]

In highlighting the need for innovation to be adopted as a practical strategy, for Africa, it is important to reflect on the changing environmental consequences.[9] Beyond building strategies innovation sustenance should be given due consideration and attention since it is about growing a system from a social, ethical and economic standpoint.[10] With the turn of events at the global level, there has been an increase in the demand for service innovation. Service driven transformations have brought about economic boom with a huge number of activities now being made up of services.[11] The effect of this upshot is that new formulas for success are now required by service innovators.[12]

Observably, at the economic level, Africa's direct investment reduced by $38 billion in 2015 against increased investments in developed economies.[13] In the light of the foregoing, it has become imperative for companies in the 21st century, to always strive to innovate. They can achieve this if they transfer their innovative thoughts from the laboratory to the broad foundation of the entire organisation. Taking the above into account, the need for firms to have a culture that supports innovation has also become imperative. Not only should companies have a culture that will enable innovation thrive, they are also obliged to nurture it across all activities in the organisation, just like a living organism.[14]

Without doubt start-ups and established companies have an opportunity to attain a new energy tradition if they develop their preference to be rejuvenated. There are two reasons deemed, to be responsible for the lack of innovation in a company; the non-existence of motivation and ineptitude of firms.[15] Innovation explicitly stresses the need for the evaluation and breaking of established rules, and calls for other activities such as going around people, to be carried out.[16] The concept under reference also presents different opportunities for social mobility and the linking of channels, with a view of commercialising discoveries that would otherwise have remained dormant.[17]

Huge investments have been made in the past towards the development of transformational innovations such as computers, biotechnology and the internet, which are today being used across the globe. Without the current application of the aforementioned innovations, it is obvious that the journey of the development of upcoming economies would have been lethargic.[18] In spite of available records of Africa's home growth,[19] the important role of innovation and industrial progression has been underplayed. It is therefore pertinent that the effect of technological reformations on economic growth be recognised and applied in the continent.[20] With a vibrant urban population and rich natural resources, Africa is judged to possess all it takes for the needed breakthrough, even though this mindset has been a captivating vision over the years.[21]

Globally, the push for innovation has continued to increase with pressure for businesses and national governments to promote it through various developmental programmes they are implementing in the regions.[22] Indeed, the evolution of the disruptive era has brought about so many changes occurring at a fast pace. In this environment, innovation plays an important function in virtually every human endeavour, making it difficult for businesses to cope or remain competitive without it.[23]

In view of the above, it has become an important responsibility of innovators to dream up the future, and then create it. What this means is that entrepreneurs should possess a good ear of discerning trifling information in addition to having sound judgment of timing.[24] From environmental observation, technologists are constantly monitoring the landscape for possible clues on the state of their technologies. While doing this, they may sometimes overlook certain signs.[25] Relating the above to customers, has revealed that satisfying them in saturated markets where expectations are high, can often lead to failures. Nevertheless, the low-cost application at the early stage of disruptive innovations, with attention on upcoming markets, is a secured approach for a breakthrough.[26]

## Learning for success

For a company that is interested in innovation, the least they should do is to have the customer always as the focus of their thoughts. What is critical in achieving this goal is the connection of the business outcomes to what customers measure as value. Doing this will determine the capabilities of the business organisation and highlight the skills to be developed or outsourced, which will generate value for customers and firms.[27] Surely, the launch of new products will abet market shares and improve the profitability of companies,[28] but a similar introduction of novel combined solutions and the contradictory introduction of capabilities will retain the traditional product identity.[29]

In consideration of the above, the new design approach for businesses should be continuous reaction to swift market changes. Applying this method would be radical and demands the incorporation of the company's goal, processes and operations.[30] Companies, investors and entrepreneurs, in place of the conventional development programmes, can adopt and implement the production of prototypes by grassroots as a worthwhile method for scaling up goods and services in markets.[31] In line with the earlier approach, economically successful countries are urged to support local economic clusters that will stimulate entrepreneurship and innovation. These local clusters should further be engaged and compete in global markets.[32] African countries on their part can secure latecomer advantages by adopting concepts such as green technologies. There is no doubt that opportunities abound for these countries if they can leapfrog the carbon lock state that appears to be stalling the developed economies[33] given that most technologies are involved in renewable power generation.[34]

Businesses determined to succeed in the competitive environment have to effectively engage their rivals together with to the rapid technological changes at the global level.[35] Accordingly, the new approach and outlook required by investors and entrepreneurs to stimulate growth is to scrutinise closely the conditions in which new ventures prosper.[36] Although new technology has been identified as a vital part of reviving companies, it is not adequate in itself. Technology should be viewed from the perspective, of being a means and tool, while its application should be suited to the processes of organisations where it functions.[37]

In the 21st century, advances in technology and other areas like transportation and new business models, have enabled companies of all sizes to function at a global scale. This globalisation of businesses has furthermore allowed companies to enter new markets once thought to be the exclusive domain of large enterprises. Following the above, large established firms strive to differentiate themselves from new competitors. In the present environment under consideration, innovation has consequently emerged as the competitive differentiator that will enable companies prove themselves as global leaders.[38] Noticeably, digital technologies have also created some new opportunities for companies to engage in. What is more, with technology, other avenues for innovation and entrepreneurship are being uncovered.[39]

For companies, competitive advantage can be achieved through the effective management and allocation of time and resources towards future innovations. On this account, sustaining innovation management is no longer considered a challenge for organisations, rather, it has been accepted as a critical driver of economic performance.[40] Indeed, the three outstanding areas that have promoted innovation and entrepreneurship at great pace are; the mobile phone, computer and the internet.[41]

It is important to restate that the culture of a company plays an important role in upholding innovation. Knowing this, newly established companies need to ascertain their value by striving to build a strong innovative culture, which comes with benefits that allow companies to attain increased efficiency of invested funds and facilitate the creation of a favourable environment. Other gains that can be derived from a company's tradition attuned to innovation, are improved products that will outdo customers.[42] Besides the listed benefits, additional rewards from crafting new business models on the basis of shifting technology, demographics and consumer habits include improved and new sources of revenue.[43] What is more, companies need to thrill their customers, protect their rising evaluation and establish their competitive advantage.[44]

In the light of the above, it is requisite for every organisation to be creative in their thoughts, and continually explore ways of understanding and making the most of rapid change.[45] Employing this, calls for an attitude that is acquiescent to new ideas.[46] Conversely, the failure of enterprises to test or think of new business concepts can be attributed to living on borrowed time.[47] Owners and leaders of businesses should aptly consider the application of innovation at all levels for their organisations if they desire to create wealth and new markets. Ideally, discovering how these businesses can craft, distribute and extract value, requires the effort of a team.[48] Without a doubt, using a systematic approach, enterprises can take on the task of creating, protecting and destroying their systems, processes and beliefs when the need arises.[49]

Another area of consideration is the creation of new business models that will result in the unleashing of ideas, passions and commitments across a company.[50] In implementing the above, consideration should be given to business models capable of leveraging technology, which, in turn, will aid the application of the innate creativity of employees. The focus of attention should be on businesses that encourage innovation and adaptability from within and across units.[51] Seeing that true innovation recognises business as a concept that stands for a number of design variables,[52] it should not be viewed as a one-off project or exception.[53]

It is pertinent at this point to highlight the related concept of value innovation and its relevance when applied. Value can be created by any organisation and its feature does not necessarily have to be technology.[54] Value is conceived only when companies align innovation with the usefulness and price of an offering. The logic of equating value and price is applicable to any business or industry, and it is also not limited to the size of a company or its worth.[55] Consequently, businesses with high growth potentials are described as those that focus strictly on value innovation to outshine their competitors rather than concentrate on outperforming or matching them.[56]

At this point, there is need to discuss the important role of technology. There are abundant examples to demonstrate how technology has influenced and shaped our lives in different ways.[57] In the area of data processing and computerisation, technology has disrupted the established customs, and this is evident in examples like smart cities and advancement in communication. The rise in the number of routine activities enabled by technology attests to the position that technology has brought about substantial practices.[58] Remarkably, the technological breakthrough of a company can be used by an innovator to create value. A perfect example is the case of Ampex, the inventor of the video tape recorder. Japanese electronics companies subsequently capitalised on the technology and developed products for the consumer market.[59] Undoubtedly, the application of the value innovation concept in to the agricultural sector as a case in point will lead to the adoption of a non-capital intensive approach.[60] Again, taking into consideration the transition in the manufacturing sector from steam-powered belts to electronically operated machines, we can get a better insight into the use and effect of technology and how it has restructured the way we work with machines.[61]

## Innovation stakeholders

Generally, the literate young population have the propensity to take advantage of modern technologies. They make the most use of telecommunication networks such as the internet, for access to information and increased learning, for instance in the area of knowledge application. Youths are also more predisposed to working for long hours and therefore more likely to engage in activities that will lead to the creation of start-ups and new products.[62] For developing countries, there are prospects for young people in the emerging area of technology model. Since these countries are not confined to the old technological system, the youths can take advantage of the new opportunities in up-and-coming and new industries.[63]

In line with the above, entrepreneurs should endeavour to use technological innovation. Any organisation that is inept in introducing innovation in the long run, stands the risk of being left behind, and its projects captured by other entities.[64] In spite of the outlined prospects and advantages of technological innovations, it must be acknowledged that they sometimes come with risks. These threats are largely connected with the possible failures of achieving the desired outcome of the application. Risks could also be seen from the perspective of the inability to build and deliver a cost-effective solution.[65]

Recognisably, seeking solutions to problems involves the endless conscious discovery and design of new and useful problems. For organisations, this implies anticipating customers' new needs and creating ways of improving offered products and services. It further entails discerning ways of improving processes and procedures while identifying opportunities to escalate the satisfaction of members within and outside the organisation.[66] With the present realities of the global competitive environment, companies cannot afford to be inactive and stay behind for everything around them to be transformed. Inaptly, many of them are sometimes overshadowed by their success or achievements and thereby lose sight of the fundamental need for them to focus their attention on the changing market conditions and customer needs.[67]

Incontestably, design and development play an important role in today's market. In an effort to stimulate demand, innovative firms are recognised for creating new markets through product design.[68] The consequence of innovation productivity will bring about the creation of a variety of products, even though these newly introduced goods may not necessarily extend the technological frontiers of the enterprise.[69] To a large extent, the size of a firm determines the prospects of innovation and affirms the view that the concept in reference varies in different types of organisations.[70] As a result of the flexible decision making advantage and malleable skills small firms have, they have proven to easily adapt to the demands of the business environment and clients. On the other hand, large enterprises may have insufficient resources to execute their innovation plans.[71]

Having discussed the significance of technology in today's market, it is important to briefly consider the interest of a critical business stakeholder; investors. Generally, the interests of investors in public companies crop up with an objective. Analysts evaluate the shares of companies based on their flexibility and consistent upgrade, in addition to their strategy in meeting their competitive challenges.[72] Since the basis of economies have moved from biological resources to intellectual, business leaders are therefore compelled to manage knowledge that is core to their organisations' achievement and development.[73] For firms to attain a leadership position ahead of their competitors, there is increasing need for them to create as their core strength, entrepreneurial processes and capabilities.[74]

In previous chapters, the concept of competition had been outlined. Nonetheless, expounding further on the relationship between skills and the competitiveness of firms, it has been established that the imitable skills and abilities of an enterprise have become the basis of their competition.[75] The point of attaining leadership position by creating core strengths and capabilities, played out in the case of Walmart, whereby the onetime famous competitive advantage position the supply chain store had, over time, became a general requirement for winning enterprises.[76] Regardless of the size and concentration of firms, the specific role of innovation in moulding the competitive environment highlights the connection between innovation and competition.[77]

With the globalisation of competition and the need to compare performances,[78] competition should not be seen as a platform for firms to destroy each other, rather, it should be regarded as a yardstick for assessing performance in innovation capacity building and growth.[79] In view of the above, the unique assets required for building a firm's competitive advantage can be achieved through the innovation- survival relationship,[80] just as the continuous flow of ideas is required to promote innovation.

For developing countries, it is not an uncommon trait for them to engage in intense competition with each other, by offering low priced goods with consequences of falling prices of products. With innovation however, the challenge of poverty and lack of food can be addressed by means of increased agricultural productivity which will lead to a reduction in the prices of food.[81] Indisputably, there is the emphasised need for a better understanding of value. The recognised elements of value that continuously grow are speed, quality, cost and convenience. These elements undergo adjustments in response to the changes in the needs of customers and what they consider important.[82] However, the solution to conquering the challenge of the rapid changing taste of customers is to frequently evaluate what they cherish.[83] A fall out of the above is the underline essential duty of an enterprise. The point to bring out here is that firms are required to establish close bonds with customers they serve, using methods such as collaboration and engagement.[84]

Again, there is need to stesss the important notion of sustaining companies' strategies. Service has been recognised as a key driver in sustaining the strategy of many companies, hence and hence, it should be upheld. A practical example of the above will give us a better understanding of how service can sustain strategy. In the case of Skype, the company encouraged service co-production with its customers.[85] The strategy of Google, a renowned world best web search provider, is also apt in illustrating the usefulness of incorporating customers into product development. The company provided additional search services for corporate clients like advertisers and content publishers for a number of income-generating, search-related services. From the onset, the developers at Google recognised the need for a new kind of server to be set up for search services. They subsequently utilised connected computers to respond quickly to each query even as innovation expanded the services of the company and enabled it to respond faster. An incremental development of the existing service, led to the success of the company.[86]

Undoubtedly applying the innovation effort will facilitate the connection of knowledge, skills, capacities and people from different perspectives.[87] Given that technology creates and maintains a network of relationships in the pursuit of new knowledge,[88] the notion of feedback, is considered a requirement for the success of innovation. The application of this concept cuts down the inherent ambiguity of the innovation process by reducing inconsistency between the market and technological sphere. Another advantage of the aforesaid notion, concept, allows for constant appraisal of the sub-processes in seeking the rationale behind decisions taken. Other areas of applying feedback is the overall performance and advancement of sub-processes[89] On account of the above, every response received from customers poses the question of how value can be better delivered in the future.[90]

The debate of shaping the local environment and making it more favourable for innovation has generated a lot of interest. In the promotion of regional innovation, public investment should be encouraged and policies that improve the establishment of clusters need to be given more attention. At the same time, the promotion of a national innovation infrastructure should also be enhanced.[91] In an economy where uncertainty is the only definite factor,[92] knowledge has been identified as the source of securing a competitive advantage. As a consequence of the above, firms' adaptability to their external environment should be closely connected to their capacity and continuous advancement of their knowledge base.[93]

Observably, there is a close link between innovation and change which organisations are supposed to use as a means of influencing their transformed environment.[94] The connection is dependent on the resources, capabilities and requirements of the organisation as transformation may involve different types of modifications.[95] The connotation of the link between innovation and change can be seen in companies that have maintained a competitive position by crafting excellent ways of scanning their environment. They quickly respond and adapt to the changing conditions in the environment, as a strategy. Albeit, achieving this requires the ability to detect environmental changes.[96]

## Stakeholders' engagement strategies

Since innovative activities in organisations are mostly controlled by the leadership of companies and employees,[97] a relationship between innovation and employment can be established. The impact of innovation on the increase in employment is, still quite minimal.[98] Whereas product innovation and high growth demand industries are inclined towards a positive employment effect, process innovation sometimes leads to job losses.[99] Given that innovation has an impact on workforce skills, it is likely to substitute inexperienced workers[100] and increase salary earnings.[101] More often than not, advances in career can be attributed to the ability of employees to creatively use the benefits of advanced technology, new information and network affiliations rather than relying on hard work.[102] In view of the effect of innovation on employment and the skills of employees, workplaces are now deliberately being planned with an emphasis on areas for teamwork. The support for individual and group impulse activities and knowledge sharing is also being given an opportunity. Team collaborative relationships now function well as a result of intense knowledge in addition to the attention and discovery opportunities it affords.[103]

Ideally, the innovation framework is not an integrated experience because the different types of innovation involve the application of diverse administrative skills. Furthermore, the nature of innovation on a product or service could make an improvement disruptive, destroy an existing product, or make it obsolete. For processes, the consequence on the production system is sometimes quite distinct from the impact of their connection to customers and markets. Beyond doubt, various types of innovation call for the application of different organisational environment with varied managerial skills.[104]

It is appropriate at this point to introduce another important system of promoting innovation at the level of the enterprise. Positively, the promotion of innovation can be expanded by employees and units within the firm through a practice termed intrapreneurship.[105] Enterprises with intrapreneurial tendencies can sustain themselves by ensuring they spend extensively on innovation just like their competitors.[106] In this instance, competition is seen as the race for breakthrough access. Building incremental improvements through the inclusion of functionality features is another means entrepreneurial firms can employ to promote innovation.[107] From the customers' perspective, incremental product improvement is sometimes more significant than a revolutionary discovered model.[108] Standing on their own, these incremental developments can be irrelevant, but when they are combined, they often turn out quite outstanding.[109] For example, the first Intel processor was slow and bulky compared to the newer versions.[110]

For conglomerates, the competition is focused on R&D efforts; therefore they cannot undo their investments in innovation.[111] These intrapreneurial conglomerates, if they have to, usually possses the enhanced ability to settle the high research and experimentation costs required to take innovation to the next level.[112] Other actions that work for the benefit of firms that should be considered include the operation of economies of scale, mass production and distribution.[113] Intrapreneurial companies further exploit their economies of scale capacity to deliver innovation to the masses through the conversion of resources to tangible assets with the capability of being traded in the market. When this is done, individual enterprises have the opportunity to make the most use of their knowledge.[114]

## Innovation promotion

Visibly around the world, national innovation strategies are being established by nations as part of their developmental plan. At the same time, countries are reforming their regulatory and tax systems to become more competitive even as they stimulate investment in information technology and improve their educational systems.[115] By kickstarting innovation across the globe, pressing economic challenges can be solved in ways that benefit individual nations and the world. The identified obstacles can be overcome by reviewing outdated and unfair policies in addition to conquering the fear of the future.[116] On the whole, the economic pressures in the world can be resolved by activating innovation in ways that nations of the world can benefit.[117]

On the part of companies, their executives can boost innovation by examining the process flow of the conversion of ideas into commercial outputs.[118] In the course of carrying out their business transactions, knowledge obtained from customers can be useful in the transformation of companies.[119] Distinctively, in the quest for external knowledge and possibilities, open communication has been recognised as an activity that should be encouraged by teams and leaders of organisations.[120] The aforesaid concept is important because it ensures a close coordination between different parts of the business. From another perspective, the core competence of a business can be developed through the collaborative efforts between different parts of the company in addition to fostering cross-functional innovation.[121] Additional intangibles that can help achieve innovation have been identified as result research, training and information technology. The usefulness of the aforementioned is perhaps the reason behind the increase in these attributes in business functions and production.[122]

It is important to highlight the active role of innovation agents in the advancement of innovation. These agents can be accelerators, incubators and financing hubs who are considered influential in the promotion of innovation. As mediators, they provide mentorship and educational components, and grant access to considerable capital, information and networking.[123]

Interestingly, in recent times, new forms of engaging science and technology for public anticipation, improvement and response to innovation have emerged.[124] Some of the contributory methods developed include drafting citizens in public decisions about research agendas, gathering views on the social and regulatory implications and requirements of certain innovations plus investment in new and emerging technologies. In spite of the successful implementation of the above, it is worthy to mention that efforts to solicit the views of organisations such as deliberate panels and citizens jury[125] have not been able to achieve much.[126]

In the face of the above conditions, the determination of the fate of companies has come to the fore. Although predicting the future is a difficult assignment to achieve, the fortunes of a company can still be ascertained and its future created. There are several cases of markets that did not exist before but were created out of pure innovation.[127] The examples of Chrysler's mini-van and CNN's 24-hour news service can be used to illustrate how new markets were created without the customers' demand for them. The needs of customers in the mentioned examples were created. Other products like the MP3 and Napster, have led new revolutions.[128]

In promoting innovation, due consideration should be given to the grassroots. A common approach of supporting innovation is embedded in the scaling up of individual initiatives identified to have potentials. This action is generally framed as going through a succession of ambitious measures to formalise and commercialise grassroots innovation. Doing this will ensure that facilities and tools of conventional innovation systems, are taken to the grassroots, for innovators to use them for their inventions. Investing in research, providing standard procedures and securing intellectual property are other ways that can be applied in formalising innovation at the grassroots.[129]

In addition to the above, a condition for grassroots innovation is the cultivation of knowledge, skills and capabilities which also double as determinants of successful outcomes. Besides the aforesaid, there are other promising measures such as working practices and community development that can be applied. By and large, finance, resources, tools, prototype facilities, imagination of participants, values and social relations can motivate people to contribute their resourcefulness towards grassroots innovation and development intentions. In circumstances where local technologies cannot be applied, efforts made can still bring about an enduring democratic value.[130] Every now and then, elites may be interested in grassroots innovation that can lead to strategic policy programmes for the support or promotion of initiatives at the local communities. This leads us to the concept of inclusive innovation which is viewed as one of several kinds of support.[131] Inclusive development involves the insertion of diversified, decentralised, and dispersed sources of solutions built by local people without external support.[132]

The inauguration of a rural innovation concept is aimed at creating an entrepreneurial culture in countrified communities for farmers to produce what they can market. This framework uses the participatory research method to reinforce the capacity of research and development partners. It also enables these developmental partners and rural communities to access early technical and market information for improved decisions by farmers.[133] In order words, rural innovation support farmers to invest in natural resources rather than deplete them for temporary market rewards.[134]

Having highlighted the advantages of innovation from communities, it is important to bring up the subject of skills required to propel it. We acknowledge that there is demand for high-quality community development skills required to facilitate community development. These talents will also be useful in articulating aspirations and needs, assisting in grassroots development and managing conflict. At the same time, they will be helpful in encouraging co-designing between ordinary people, for new infrastructure that works for them. The establishment of community workshops can also facilitate the achievement of the above. This process of introducing community workshops and making them legitimately available can be challenging. Nevertheless, it is easier to have them rather than allow individuals have personal operated ones with the view that it is for the neighbourhood.[135] There are examples of community development programmes found in cities like Barcelona and São Paulo. Authorities here have invested in the creation of public fablabs where citizens can be engaged in digital design and construction.[136] They have further established training institutions where machine tools are made available to grassroots groups at flexible hours.[137] Notably, these community development programmes cannot be achieved without the integration of diversified solutions sourced from individuals with varied proficiency and spread across local communities.[138]

Overall, because the globalisation of the world has impacted greatly on the nature of competition, promoting innovation in the rural areas or grassroots has a general implication for the innovation of the nation. Grassroots innovations emerge when existing systems and practices fail to serve people's needs. They can happen by chance, organised experimentation, or by merging solutions in new ways. The creation of organisations that foster grassroots innovation will, amongst other things, expand the public pool of innovation by providing financial motivation to innovators. This incentive will attract them to the programme and reduce the barriers to diffusion. Other methods that can be used to enhance grassroots innovation have been identified.

The investment in children's ideas should be part of the innovation promotion initiative, given that their ideas are known to have viable solutions embedded in them. By experience, children approach problems imaginatively. Young persons by nature sometimes find creative solutions from other perspectives that adults may not consider. Relatedly, as part of developing grassroots innovation, university students can be organised to proffer solutions to social problems as a segment of their graduate programmes. To this end, relevant platforms should be created to facilitate collaboration, and continuous problem-solving activities.[139]

The development of grassroots innovation has also helped to uncover various opportunities that groups can take advantage of.[140] In the light of the above, the advancement of innovation in our communities is critical. Furthermore, support for the subject can also take the outline of creating workshops at the local levels, to motivate innovators to share their work and foster collaboration. It can also be in the form of building fabrication workshops and locating them in the homes of innovators, for access to machinery and tools that otherwise would be difficult to obtain within their immediate environment.[141]

The economic growth of African countries has been ephemeral as a result of the reliance of their global competitiveness on inexpensive labour. These countries further contend with each other by offering cut-rate goods, which give rise to reducing prices. Without a doubt, innovation can be used to grow and sustain Africa's economy.[142] Taking a cue from some developing countries in Asia, the significance of innovation in the development of countries like Singapore and South Korea should be considered. Innovation-driven effort has brought about an improvement in their growth rate, but, this is not without the important contributions of their institutions.[143]

As a result of the demand for the development of sustainable innovation in Africa, environmentally friendly modes of economic production and consumption should be offered. To support the earlier point made, an alternative model of sustainable development that is driven by innovation is required to scale up and overcome the traditional fossil-fuelled industrial model.[144] Indeed, there are great potentials for the application of energy-efficient services to most part of Africa as an alternative fuel, particularly in areas such as transportation and power co-generation, while industrial systems can equally be built from the harnessed renewable energy resources. The earlier highlighted concept of development driven by innovation has the capability of being sold, besides assisting in achieving developmental objectives.[145]

National bounded innovation systems can also enhance innovation,[146] just as agencies like government ministries and financial institutions can impact on the effectiveness of innovation. Consequently having a national approach in policy thinking is important, although drawing analytical boundaries around the national systems alone can create a challenge because boundaries that identify exact systems are vague.[147] It should be pointed out that the innovation efficiency of a national system is dependent on the gains and rewards from trading on the output of innovation.[148]

The creation of an active global innovation economy, calls for an international innovation policy framework.[149] Consequently, the successful application of a nation's innovation capacity in its economic activities is necessary for the attainment of sustainable development and the extension of peoples' capabilities.[150] Regrettably, some African countries have been classified as having a shortage of innovation competences, with implications for capacity failure[151] which is considered more serious than market failure.[152] The growth of the continent however can be strengthened by the capacity of countries within to incorporate and effectively use knowledge and technology instead of focusing on building up capital, aid dependency and a stable macroeconomic environment.[153]

In the light of the above, policymakers in Africa must surmount the challenge of harnessing technologies and innovation to meet the needs of the diverse growing population. In the health sector, for instance, innovation can be used to address the challenges being faced.[154] Concerning firms, the decision to invest in innovation to a large extent is dependent on their post-innovation returns, hence making it an important element to be outlined.

The post-innovation returns are reliant on the capacities of firms and their market environment.[155] Sometimes, these returns determine the decision taken by firms to invest in innovation. Decisions to make include the choice and nature of innovation the firm should invest in while related issues for consideration take account of the type of innovation to be carried out – whether radical or incremental, as well as the risks involved in engaging in the innovation activity. Furthermore, the technological complication of the project, sales and profitability potentials are factors to be reflected upon.[156]

Given the importance of policy in the advancement of innovation, it is pertinent to emphasise that nations do not get it wrong. Countries should strive to create a wholesome innovation system with a focus on win-win innovations. It would be beneficial to most countries if a global race for innovation initiative is implemented. This initiative would help attain increased productivity in the area of improved products and services as well as revenues. However, launching such a laudable programme would come with some challenges.[157] Certainly, there is need for African countries to focus on improving their knowledge economy and expand their institutional framework towards the achievement of the established goals.[158] By strengthening the information system, new knowledge and technology can be sourced and applied to improve innovation in various sectors.[159]

## Conclusion

The connection between the low rate of innovation and institutional development is evident in some African countries while others have enhanced their innovative output through established institutions.[160] Without a doubt, agriculture and agro-industries are critical sectors in most African economies,[161] with a contribution of 34% to GDP.[162] Due to the criticality of the aforementioned sectors, innovation can play an important role in generating improvements, by way of increasing yields[163] which will subsequently address hunger and malnutrition problems being faced by some countries. Indeed, the business of agricultural growth is a burning interest for policymakers, agric-business owners and other stakeholders[164] particularly because the development of this sector is an effective way of reducing poverty.[165]

The preceding chapter talked about innovation democracy and its value in promoting grassroots innovation. Reiterating the importance of this concept, innovation democracy emphasises the ability of people to confront the path of innovation for every community to be involved in the process and be empowered.[166] Applying this concept underscores the need for public administration. As the state provides the legal framework for intellectual property rights, it is also accountable for research funds and training of personnel.[167] Democracy in innovation is very important as in other areas of public life[168] and part of the entitlements of innovation democracy requires the building of laboratories from partnerships.[169]

In sum, innovation can be achieved by the investments in intangibles such as employee training, information technology, customer acquisition and so on. This will lead to a rise in production assets and functions of businesses.[170] Above all, it has been established that partnerships can improve the rate of innovation. These partnerships can be between formal and informal science groups. Take for example the natural product laboratory, Sadbhav-SRISTI-Sanshodhan, which was created over a decade ago through a grant from a private philanthropist in Mumbai. This partnership works on ideas, innovations and traditional knowledge of people in various areas such as veterinary, and agriculture.[171]

There is no doubt that successful engagement between the formal and informal sectors can be achieved if they are recognised and respected while the reward of creative grassroots knowledge systems can also facilitate successful partnerships.[172]

## Notes

1  Bartes (2009); Senge (2007). Barták (2006).
2  Weiser (2011).
3  Assink (2006).
4  Madrid-Guijarro, Garcia and Van Auken (2009). Oyelaran-Oyeyinka, Laditan and Esubiyi (1996); Tulus and Hamonangan (2011).
5  Hamel (2003).
6  Assink (2006).
7  Hart (1995).
8  Urbancova (2013).
9  Hart (1995).
10 Steiner (2006).
11 Bartes (2009); Hamel and Green (2007); Senge, (2007).
12 Assink (2006).
13 Christensen, Ojomo and Van Bever (2017).
14 Shapiro (2003), Gilbert (2003), Kooskora (2004), von Hippel (1988), Baumol (2011).
15 Shapiro (2003).
16 Shapiro (2003).
17 Eyal-Cohen (2019).
18 Atkinson and Ezell (2013).
19 Christensen, Ojomo and Van Bever (2017).
20 Atkinson and Ezell (2013).
21 Christensen, Ojomo and Van Bever (2017).
22 Kooskora (2004).
23 Kooskora (2004).
24 Gilbert (2003).
25 Bustinza, Gomes, Vendrell-Herrero and Baines (2019).
26 Urbancova (2013).
27 Shapiro (2003).
28 Urbancova (2013).
29 Bustinza, Gomes, Vendrell-Herrero and Baines (2019).
30 Weiser (2011).
31 Smith and Stirling (2016).
32 Weiser (2011).
33 Mathews (2013).
34 Lee, Juma and Mathews (2014).
35 Kooskora (2004).
36 Christensen, Ojomo and Van Bever (2017).
37 Shapiro (2003).
38 McLaughlin and Caraballo (2013).
39 Coulson-Thomas (2017).
40 Andreessen, 2011

41  Weiser (2011).
42  Urbancova (2013).
43  Assink (2006).
44  Urbancova (2013).
45  Kiely (1993).
46  Kiely (1993).
47  Hamel (2003).
48  Hamel (2003).
49  Kandampully (2002).
50  Hamel (2003).
51  Shapiro (2003).
52  Hamel (2003).
53  Hamel (2003).
54  Dillon, Lee and Matheson (2005).
55  Jacobs and Zulu (2012).
56  Kim and Mauborgne (1997).
57  Smith and Stirling (2016).
58  Smith and Stirling (2016).
59  Dillon, Lee and Matheson (2005).
60  Jacobs and Zulu (2012).
61  Smith and Stirling (2016).
62  Ojeaga (2015).
63  Freeman and Soete (1985); Perez and Soete (1988).
64  Urbancova (2013).
65  Åstebro and Michela (2005).
66  Shapiro (2003).
67  Johnson and Kirchain (2011).
68  Aghion, Howitt and Bursztyn (2010).
69  Aghion, Howitt and Bursztyn (2010).
70  Hoffman, Parejo, Bessant and Perren (1998).
71  Urbancova (2013).
72  Shapiro (2003).
73  Hansen, Nohria and Tierney (1999).
74  Shapiro (2003).
75  Assink (2006).
76  Cantwell (2005).
77  Assink (2006).
78  Cantwell (2005).
79  Krugman (1994).
80  Esteve-Pérez and Mañez-Castillejo (2008).
81  Juma (2011).
82  Shapiro (2003).
83  Shapiro (2003).
84  Shapiro (2003).
85  Assink (2006).
86  Assink (2006).
87  Usher (1954); von Hippel (1988).
88  Kandampully (2002).
89  Usher, (1954); von Hippel (1988).
90  Shapiro (2003).

91  Porter and Stern (2001).
92  Nonaka, (1991).
93  Johannessen, Olaisen and Olsen (1999).
94  Damanpour (1991).
95  Baregheh, Rowley and Sambrook (2009).
96  Shapiro (2003).
97  Urbancova (2013).
98  Pianta (2005).
99  Vivarelli, Evangelista and Pianta (1996).
100  Acemoglu, D. (2002).
101  Kandampully (2002).
102  Andreessen (2011).
103  Assink (2006).
104  Eyal-Cohen (2019).
105  Baumol (2011).
106  Baumol (2011).
107  Gladwell (2011).
108  Gladwell (2011).
109  Gladwell (2011).
110  Eyal-Cohen (2019).
111  Baumol (2011).
112  Eyal-Cohen (2019).
113  Eyal-Cohen (2019).
114  Atkinson and Ezell (2013).
115  Atkinson and Ezell (2013).
116  Atkinson and Ezell (2013).
117  Hansen and Birkinshaw (2007).
118  Shapiro (2003).
119  Barlow (2007).
120  Shapiro (2003).
121  Lev (2001).
122  Eyal-Cohen (2019).
123  Callon, Lascoumes and Barthe (2009).
124  Smith and Stirling (2016).
125  Levidow (1998).
126  Smith and Stirling (2016).
127  Shapiro (2003).
128  Smith and Stirling (2016).
129  Smith and Stirling (2016).
130  OECD (2015).
131  Richards (1998).
132  Kaaria, Sanginga, Njuki, Delve, Chitsike and Best (2009).
133  Best and Kaganzi (2003).
134  Smith and Stirling (2016).
135  Smith and Stirling (2016).
136  Smith and Stirling (2016).
137  Gupta (2013).
138  Basadur, Runco and VEGAxy (2000).
139  Gupta (2013).
140  Ketels (2008); Miron (2010); Mudambi and Swift (2012).

141 Smith and Stirling (2016).
142 Juma (2011).
143 Christensen, Ojomo and Van Bever (2017).
144 Lee, Juma and Mathews (2014).
145 Lee, Juma and Mathews (2014).
146 Meyer (2013).
147 Metcalfe and Ramlogan (2008).
148 Oluwatobi, Efobi, Olurinola and Alege (2015).
149 Atkinson and Ezell (2013).
150 Lee, Juma and Mathews (2014).
151 Lee, Juma and Mathews (2014).
152 Nelson (1993); Lundvall (1992); Metcalfe (2005).
153 Onyeiwu, (2015).
154 Kalua, Awotedu, Kamwanja and Saka (2009).
155 Du, Love and Roper (2007).
156 Lavado and Cabrera (2008). Keizer and Halman (2007).
157 Atkinson and Ezell (2013).
158 Mahagaonkar (2008).
159 Jacobs and Zulu (2012).
160 Oluwatobi, Efobi, Olurinola and Alege (2015).
161 Eyal-Cohen (2019).
162 Juma (2011).
163 Lee, Juma and Mathews (2014).
164 Jacobs and Zulu (2012).
165 Juma (2011).
166 Kaaria, Sanginga, Njuki, Delve, Chitsike and Best (2009).
167 Mazzucato (2011).
168 Smith and Stirling (2016).
169 Mazzucato (2011).
170 Lev (2001).
171 Gupta (2013).
172 Gupta (2013).

# 6 Taking the next steps

## Introduction

In order to acquire new customers, companies are urged to speedily improve their innovative capacities in the face of increasing global competition.[1] The satisfaction and fulfilment of customers' needs will be determined by the products and services companies offer. Basically, there are three stakeholders that decide the innovativeness of a product, namely: the company, consumer and the society. In designing products therefore, consideration should be given to the needs, values and goals of the above-mentioned stakeholders. When this is done, it will bring about an overall understanding of the definition of the innovative product.[2] Today, the concept of quality is judged as a basic requirement and core offering by customers and no longer a competitive tool for enterprises.[3]

It has been established that innovative ideas are generated from all parts of an organisation. Innovation can further originate from the internal interface beyond the boundaries of a firm. Regardless of where an idea originates from, the important thing to note is that knowledge is essential for innovation creation.[4] As a result, wherever opportunities exist for information and new knowledge to be accessed becomes a potential source of innovation. Like other types of knowledge, innovative ideas[5] are also dispersed in informal networks, which can sometimes bring about challenges. Just now, the traditional approach of managing individual actions and behaviours when knowledge resides in employees is limited, whereas accessing resident knowledge of social networks is a more viable approach. A proper understanding and participation in networks where innovative ideas are derived from is essential.[6]

## Economic development and competition

The objective of creating an impact in the lives of people is an impelling force for an organisation's dedication and steadfastness. If the desired impact is huge, the firm would require overwhelming commitment. What this infers for businesses is that, in competing for the future, the prospects of creating an impression for customers is what is important and not the assurance of immediate financial gains.[7] Obviously, the basis of competition has now been redefined. It is now between dawdlers and challengers. Those described as laggards would follow at best the path with the least resistance. On the contrary, the latter described category are people who generally look towards developing more resourceful solutions to address customer problems. Furthermore, these contenders are more unconventional than incumbents in new solutions that emerge. The challenge in the business environment is viewed as a contest between incumbents and innovators. Viewed from another perspective, competition is also seen as inaction versus the imaginative. The example of discount warehouse shopping versus the traditional departmental store drives home the understanding of the nature of competition described above. Here, the challengers were more unconventional than the contenders in the new solution that evolved. It is evident from the above that the new characteristic of competition now aims for the maximisation of the quota of opportunity that a firm can access within an extensive area.[8]

With the turn of events at the international level, it is the responsibility of nations to support the creation of industries of the future; otherwise, they will be misplaced in their economic standing. An additional contractual obligation of countries is the protection of existing industries.[9] As active players, firms can, on their part, avert being bystanders in the market by taking action and participating actively in the path to the future. The effective involvement of companies necessitates them attuning their values and skills to the ever-changing state of affairs of their industries.[10] These firms are further expected to devote time to reflect on the outlook of competition. As part of the strategy, team members should confer on the objective of building a deep shared view of the future, to obtain a more distinct analysis from the process.[11]

A practical illustration of the importance of the above is the case of the Swiss watch manufacturers who, at a point in time, produced nearly 65% of all watches made in the world and obtained about 90% of the market's profit. Although they invented the gear system and their products improved and maintained superior standards, they still lost their leadership position in the industry. The reason for the leadership displacement was because they failed to anticipate changes in the demands of their customers and did not innovate to meet up with the new needs.[12] On the other hand, Swatch, another player in the industry, was able to foresee that customers would have other reasons for wearing a wristwatch beyond telling the time. They therefore focused their attention on selling costume jewelleries to suit the prevailing lifestyle of customers. With a 10% market share against the 35% of Japanese manufacturers, the Swiss lost their dominance of the industry.[13] It is essential for firms to recognise that as they strive to be market leaders, the attitude to exhibit should be from the standpoint that a strategy that worked previously may not necessarily apply in the future.[14]

## Driving innovation

Certainly, there is need for entrepreneurs and companies to bear in mind that technological changes are quick and regularly discontinuous, thereby leading to reduced product life cycles.[15] The rule of modern business, of course, has been modified from finding needs and filling them to imagining needs and creating them.[16] The effect of changes in global business has also influenced the type of attitude to be adopted. The appropriate mindset for business has now moved beyond discovering new solutions to meeting customers' needs, necessitating keenness and the willingness to look far beyond the old.[17] Right now, with the global turn of events, the question that firms need to respond to should be: how can potential opportunities be acquired with current skills and competences? Another related enquiry that should be examined is how the current capabilities can be built for the enterprise to capture a large percentage of their future market. In answering the above questions, the prerequisite action required is to first undertake an analysis of the deficient skills, followed by articulating those to be developed in addition to understanding the changing nature of competition. Besides, these actions, there is also the need to also improve the position of the enterprise in the market.[18]

Incontestably, the imminent success of businesses has been replaced with vying for maximum opportunity they can access as opposed to the pursuit of market share.[19] It has been earlier established in previous chapters that the long term sustainability of a firm relies on its resolute ability to regularly tackle the changing market and economic environment.[20] Companies have to operate from the perspective of competing for opportunities with the recognised disposition of technological changes like the internet that has transformed the world.[21] Having highlighted the new direction of competition in the business environment, it should be emphasised that firms do not work in seclusions, rather they should work in cross-functional teams,[22] especially as the knowledge to innovate is globally dispersed.[23] This notion of intersect teams working together is supported by the open innovation concept where external and internal ideas are made use of in the paths to markets.[24]

Inquisitively, some questions border on the path of innovation, the competitive advantage of a business, as well as the type of customers that services should be offered to. Answering these questions will set in motion the realisation of the importance of innovation in a business enterprise.[25] Having the above mindset clearly has become essential, particularly in the face of persistent competitive demands arising from trade globalisation. The current reality now is for firms to rely more on constant innovation of products, processes and organisational designs for their continued existence and growth.[26] Bearing in mind the inevitable necessity of satisfying clients anticipation has increasingly become the process of customer direction into the future for businesses. Thus, thinking for the customer and pre-empting their future needs is considered a foremost approach for attaining superiority in business.[27] On the other hand, failure to foresee and partake in the opportunities of the future can lead to the impoverishment of firms and nations.[28] The point to take is that the future should not only be envisaged or visualised, it should also be built.[29]

A relevant practical illustration that will help drive the importance of imagining the future needs of customers is the notion of strategic architecture where the profession of the architect is used to explain how customers demands can be created. Foreseeing a structure and designing it into a blueprint requires a combination of art and structural engineering. Applying the techniques implored by the architect in the business environment would bring about tremendous benefits. Beyond companies, we can also extend the strategic architectural concept to the level of nations.[30] Undeniably, it is appropriate for countries to have a strategic architectural plan in place even if it is not a detailed one. Clearly, it will help identify the capabilities required to be built by the country and spell out how this can be done. Apart from highlighting the competencies to be acquired, the concept under reference will also provide guidance and outline deliberate steps to be taken towards achieving economic development of the country. Singapore, for instance, had a tactical design plan drafted by the country's economic development board. The plan outlined the proficiencies of the nation and those to be acquired towards the attainment of industrial development.[31] We can see innovation can be premeditated and managed in order to take control of an organisation's potential resources.[32] To achieve this, the organisation requires a definite framework.[33]

Further consideration of the subject, innovation, also highlights the role of communication in the process. These two concepts – communication and innovation – should go with other tangibles like culture and trust. The importance of culture in promoting innovation has already been highlighted in previous chapters. The listed intangibles of culture and trust are not easily measured and managed[34] but are directly dependent on the effective communication of the enterprise.[35] This is true and applicable not only for individual corporations but the entire ecosystem as well. Adequate or lack of communication is more apparent whenever information correlated to intangibles is absent. When this occurs, it can negatively affect the business operations and management by the influence of stakeholders.[36]

### Open innovation systems and knowledge sharing

Within an ecosystem, connections have to be maintained and a cordial culture cultivated.[37] Since the ecosystem requires information dissemination for its survival, communication has become an essential element for the system to thrive.[38] The role of communication as pointed out will facilitate the exchange of ideas particularly in an ecosystem.[39] It should be recognised that if ideas cannot flow freely, the goal of sharing information cannot be achieved. Incontestably, the interest in communication within the ecosystem has increased because of the effect of its functionality on the structure.[40] It therefore follows that the success of businesses, more than ever before, is directly dependent on the effective communication of the enterprise.[41]

In sustaining development and retaining market competitiveness, managers and employees must realise that the success of their organisations in the future may not be based on their current knowledge and experience. Accordingly, they need to be true to themselves that these capabilities may in fact become irrelevant or obsolete in the future. Given that countries have to contend with factors such as cross border mobility, educational underdevelopment and lack of infrastructure, it is obvious that there has been a scarcity of talents across the world.[42] Observably, the social sustenance of development is not as simple as it appears, rather, it is getting more complex mostly as it relates to innovation development. This is also primarily because innovation is not only concerned with the development of new and appropriate solutions, it also entails the destruction of previous solutions[43] that are directly or indirectly associated with people, users and creators.[44]

Certainly, sourcing for innovation requires us to scan the external environment for capabilities and processes that will enable us create and commercialise technology. It will also help us promote innovation while being focused on conventional thinking. The example of Israel readily comes to mind to demonstrate the above point. The country's success in innovation is attributed to the conducive environment it had. Factors such as strong university and connection with experts like scientists and engineers contributed immensely to the development of innovation.[45] While the innovation system is characterised by complex relationships among stakeholders such as universities and research institutes,[46] for its success, it requires the exchange of technology and information among people, enterprises and institutions.[47]

In general, human and material resources have also been identified as actors in the system. Characteristically, students and researchers make up the human resources, while the material resources include funds, equipment and facilities amongst others.[48] Other participating actors of the ecosystem that play a crucial role include institutions such as universities, colleges, business schools and policymakers.[49]

Undoubtedly, the promotion of innovation in Africa can be resolved by the adoption and implementation of the open innovation ecosystem which is described as a system with an open space where technology can be used by large organisations, start-ups and students who have come together, to create business solutions that will stand the test of time. The above concept was espoused from three research areas of innovation namely: open innovation, lean innovation and innovation labs, and tailored from the innovation ecosystem at the *Singularity University*.[50] Expanding further on the above-mentioned research areas, the innovation lab is described as an unrestrictive creative environment whereby individuals can venture into developing something original, exclusive and unanticipated, with the ability of breaking recognised organisational models. This laboratory is, however, not equipped to scale up successful innovations.[51] On the other hand, the Singularity University (SU) is an open innovation campus where high-tech is used by large enterprises, start-ups and innovators to create new business solutions. Entrepreneurial teams, groups from large organisations, teams as well as field impact partners are motivated to stimulate disruptive innovation by proceeding quickly from ideas to models. The campus referred to here assembles people from different fields all over the world with a shared vision.[52]

The open innovation ecosystem is a relatively harmless playing field for innovative thinkers to explore while its application will enhance the innovative capacity and procedure of achieving systematic execution of the innovation space.[53] There is no doubt that actors in the ecosystem have a functional goal which is to facilitate innovation and technological development. It is important to point out that the system models the economic rather than active energy of intricate relationships created between participants and entities which can be carried out through private, government or straight investments by businesses.[54] Since the symbol of ecosystem stems from the inter-relations of players within, it is obvious that actors cannot succeed independently. Recognisably, interaction within the system can be temporary or permanent, or it can take the form of exchange of ideas amongst actors to facilitate innovation.[55] Quite a number of attributes of the system are intangible[56] while capital in the context of the inno-vation ecosystem includes skills of employees, tacit and market knowl-edge. Others include reputation, formal and informal social networks, patents and brands.[57]

The availability of resources is also an important area of considera-tion for the innovation ecosystem. These resources are tied with those created by the commercial economy as a fraction of their profits. Yet another characteristic of the ecosystem is the geographical location of actors within a system. In other words, members are either physically localised, or linked strategically with attention on developing specific technology. The renowned Silicon Valley is a good illustration of a geographical or localised ecosystem.[58] Investment in human capital as well as the provision of subsistence means within the system are meas-ures of attracting and engaging champions.[59] Viewed differently, eco-systems also benefit from the effective engagement of average growing enterprises who were once considered unsuccessful by venture capi-talists as a result of their unappealing profits.[60] Overall, innovations are recognised as the outcome of ecosystems, made up of vibrant multi-processes and connections including researchers, entrepreneurs, experts, legislators.[61] The operation of the ecosystem stimulates inno-vation and the communication of partners in their areas of expertise, with the objective of supporting and strengthening the system.[62]

## The role of partnerships

Indeed, the goal of a transformation process is resourcefulness, but the outcome of the implementation result can occasionally be evolu-tionary. Over time, some development opportunities will prove to be radical. Since the future is not an extrapolation of the past, we expect that old industrial structures will be overtaken by new structures. Ex-clusive markets are also expected to be transformed into mass markets in the future even as some leading edge scientific discoveries will be converted eventually to conventional household appliances.[63] In the light of the above, companies with interest in creating the future, see things from the perspective of generating revenue from the potential customer benefits they perceive. Failure to do this will threaten their leadership position and erode their market shares.

With the outcome of the above, leadership is increasingly getting to the stage where it will be measured by the capacity to act rather than think. Sadly, many companies that were leaders in the past did not retain their leadership position.[64] In consideration of the aforesaid, there are a number partnerships that can be imitated. The partnership involving Techshop, a fabrication studio, BMW and UnternehmerTUM readily comes to mind. The outcome of their partnership brought about a high-tech workshop that was targeted at business founders, start-ups and employees, but made available for the public to access.[65] Innovators used the space and facilities provided by the Techshop to realise their ideas.[66]

Recognisably, China developed its innovative strength from partnership with other countries. Although the country was not a technological leader from an innovative and competitive perspective, she however built strong alliances with foreign countries in key areas, and her innovative strength consequently developed over time.[67] The outcome of the Chinese partnerships has led to an increase in innovation and also brought about new technologies, businesses and models. Clearly, with a swing from the old to the new momentum, elements such as e-commerce and mobile payment have been facilitated.[68] Reflecting on the challenges being faced by many countries, we observe how a number of them who were previously industry leaders at a point in time, failed to keep up with the increasing pace of transformation in the industry.[69] Examples of companies that were affected by changes in their industries within the last decade include General Motors and Sears who were respectively incumbent leaders in the automobile and clothing industries in the United States at a time.[70] The two listed companies relied on successive generation of their customers to continue using their products and services. Sears, for instance assumed that future customers in rural America would kit themselves and their homes conveniently using their catalogue. On the part of General Motors, the company was sure that customers in the future would be satisfied and as their income increased, the young customers would keep using their brands or trade the old models (Buicks) for new ones (Cadillacs) just as their parents did.[71]

## Conclusion

Although some enterprises are fully concerned with the services they offer in their bid to satisfy customers, from the standpoint of the customers however, what they are interested in is how these firms offer their services to them rather than the services being offered focus of firms.[72] The difference between the changes in the environment whereby a company is operating and its internal setting, generates an organisational transformation challenge. Importantly, transformation initiatives such as downsizing, overhead reduction, employee empowerment, process design are not sufficient to restore the leadership position of firms. Even though these listed adjustments may not disrupt the future in a competitive contest, they can however be combined with other methods suited for innovation breakthrough.[73] Furthermore, conventional business reorganisation programmes like lean six sigma can stimulate creativity they are not the most appropriate for identifying breakthrough innovation ideas.[74]

The assurance that African countries can, in spite of the current level of knowledge economy, have the propensity to catch up with other countries within a time frame, based on the stance of rationalisation, is relevant.[75] Therefore, an acceptable requirement for innovation is the successful actualisation of customers' reward.[76]

## Notes

1 OECD (2013).
2 Tan and McAloone (2006).
3 Kandampully (1996).
4 Howells (2002).
5 Tsoukas (1996).
6 Björk and Magnusson (2009).
7 Hamel and Prahalad (1994).
8 Hamel and Prahalad (1994).
9 Hamel and Prahalad (1994).
10 Hamel and Prahalad (1994).
11 Hamel and Prahalad (1994).
12 Hoerl and Gardner (2010).
13 Jay and Ria (1999).
14 Jay and Ria (1999).
15 Achrol (1991).
16 Jay and Ria (1999).
17 Hamel and Prahalad (1994).
18 Hamel and Prahalad (1994).
19 Hamel and Prahalad (1994).
20 Basadur (2004).
21 Luoma-aho and Halonen (2010).
22 Owens and Fernandez (2014).
23 Singularity (2014).
24 Chesbrough (2003a) Chesbrough (2003b).

25  Hamel and Prahalad (1994).
26  Luoma-aho and Halonen (2010).
27  Jay and Ria (1999).
28  Hamel and Prahalad (1994).
29  Hamel and Prahalad (1994).
30  Hamel and Prahalad (1994).
31  Hamel and Prahalad (1994).
32  Prahalad (1993).
33  Jay and Ria (1999).
34  Lev (2001).
35  Malmelin (2007).
36  Lev (2001).
37  Luoma-aho and Halonen (2010).
38  Ruppel and Harrington (2000).
39  Estrin (2009).
40  Mast, Huck and Zerfas (2005).
41  Malmelin (2007).
42  Hamel and Prahalad (1994).
43  Schumpeter (1980).
44  Steiner (2006).
45  Porter and Stern (2001).
46  Ander (2006).
47  Kirner, SpomenkaMaloca, Rogowski, Slama, Oliver Som, Spitzley and Wagner (2007).
48  Deborah (2011).
49  Deborah (2011).
50  Böhmer and Lindemann (2015).
51  Böhmer and Lindemann (2015).
52  Böhmer and Lindemann (2015).
53  Böhmer and Lindemann (2015).
54  Deborah (2011).
55  Jansen, Van Den Bosch and Volbera (2006).
56  Kaplan and Norton (2004).
57  Contractor (2000).
58  Deborah (2011).
59  Deborah (2011).
60  Estrin (2009).
61  Estrin (2009).
62  Zheng (2013).
63  Hamel and Prahalad (1994).
64  Wienstroth (2013).
65  Hamel and Prahalad (1994).
66  Wienstroth (2013).
67  Böhmer and Lindemann (2015).
68  Lee, Juma and Mathews (2014).
69  Hamel and Prahalad (1994).
70  Hamel and Prahalad (1994).
71  Hamel and Prahalad (1994).
72  Hamel and Prahalad (1994).

73 Jay and Ria (1999).
74 Hoerl and Gardner (2010).
75 Asongu (2013).
76 Watty (2013); Binz and Reichle (2005).

# References

Aarikka-Stenroos, L., Jaakkola, E., Harrison, D., and Mäkitalo-Keinonen, T. (2017). How to manage innovation processes in extensive networks: A longitudinal study. *Industrial Marketing Management*, 67, 88–105.

Aarikka-Stenroos, L., & Sandberg, B. (2012). From new-product development to commercialization through networks. *Journal of Business Research*, 65(2), 198–206.

Acemoglu, D. (2002). Technical change, inequality, and the labor market. *Journal of Economic Literature*, 40(1), 7–72.

Achrol, R. S. (1991). Evolution of the marketing organization: New forms for turbulent environments. *Journal of Marketing*, 55(4), 77–93.

Adams, K. (2005). The Sources of Innovation and Creativity. Paper commissioned by the National Center on Education and the Economy for the New Commission on the Skills of the American Workforce. Washington, DC: National Center on Education and the Economy

Aghion, P., Howitt, P., and Bursztyn, L. (2010). L'économie de la croissance. *Economica*. Paris.

Allen, T. J. (1977). *Managing the Flow of Technology*. Cambridge, MA: MIT Press.

Alm, H., and McKelvey, M. (2000). When and why does cooperation positively or negatively affect innovation? An exploration into turbulent waters, Discussion Paper 39, Centre for Research on Innovation and Competition (CRIC), Manchester, November 2000.

Amabile, T. M. (1998). *How to Kill Creativity (Vol. 87)*. Boston, MA: Harvard Business School Publishing.

Amit, R., and Schoemaker, P. J. (1993). Strategic assets and organizational rent. *Strategic Management Journal*, 14(1), 33–46.

Ander, R. (2006). Match your innovation strategy to your innovation ecosystem. *Harvard Business Review*, 84, 98–107.

Andreessen, M. (2011). Why software is eating the world. *Wall Street Journal*, 20, C2.

Andrews, K. R. (1971). *Concept of corporate strategy*. Homewood, IL: Irwin.

Asheim, B. T., and Gertler, M. S. (2005). The geography of innovation – Regional innovation systems, in J. Fagerberg, D. C. Mowery and R. R. Nelson (eds.), *The Oxford Handbook of Innovation*. Oxford: Oxford University Press, 291–317.

Assink, M. (2006). Inhibitors of disruptive innovation capability: A conceptual model. *European Journal of Innovation Management*, 9, 215–233.

Asongu, S. (2013). Modeling the future of knowledge economy: Evidence from SSA and MENA countries. *Economics Bulletin*, 33(1), 612–624.

Åstebro, T., and Michela, J. L. (2005). Predictors of the survival of innovations. *Journal of Product Innovation Management*, 22(4), 322.

Atkinson, R. D., and Ezell, S. J. (2013). Building the global innovation economy. *The Futurist*, 47(1), 14.Audretsch, D. B., Lehmann, E. E., and Warning, S. (2005). University spillovers and new firm location. *Research Policy*, 34, 1113–1122.

Audretsch, D. B., & Stephan, P. E. (1996). Company-scientist locational links: The case of biotechnology. *The American Economic Review*, 86(3), 641–652.

Baas, T., and Schrooten, M. (2006). Relationship banking and SMEs: A theoretical analysis. *Small Business Economics*, 27(2–3), 127–137.

Baiyere, A., and Roos, J. (2011). Disruptive innovations at the bottom of the pyramid: Can they impact on the sustainability of today's companies?. *Trends and Future of Sustainable Development*, 40, 134–140.

Baker, W. E., and Sinkula, J. M. (2002). Market orientation, learning orientation and product innovation: Delving into the organization's black box. *Journal of Market-focused Management*, 5(1), 5–23.

Bakker, H., Boersma, K., and Oreel, S. (2006). Creativity (ideas) management in industrial R&D organizations: A crea-political process model and an empirical illustration of Corus RD&T. *Creativity and Innovation Management*, 15(3), 296–309.

Baregheh, A., Rowley, J., and Sambrook, S. (2009). Towards a multidisciplinary definition of innovation. *Management Decision*, 47(8), 1323–1339.

Barlow, C. M. (2007). Thinking more effectively about deliberate innovation. *Howe School Alliance for Technology Management*, 11(1), 1–8.

Barták, J. (2006). *Skryté bohatství firmy*. Praha: Alfa.

Bartes, F. (2009). *Paradigma inovací a hodnotové inženýrství*. Brno: VÚT.

Basadur, M. (2004). Leading others to think innovatively together: Creative leadership. *The Leadership Quarterly*, 15(1), 103–121.

Basadur, M. I. N., Runco, M. A., and VEGAxy, L. A. (2000). Understanding how creative thinking skills, attitudes and behaviors work together: A causal process model. *The Journal of Creative Behavior*, 34(2), 77–100.

Baumol, W. J. (2010). *The Microtheory of Innovative Entrepreneurship*. New Jersey: Princeton University Press.

Bayh, B., and Allen, J. P. (2012). School power: The case for keeping innovation in the hands of universities. *The Atlantic*, 11

Bessant, J., and Tidd, J. (2009). *Inovação e empreendedorismo*. Porto Alegre: Bookman Editora..

Best, R., and Kaganzi, E. (2003). Farmer participation in market research to identify income-generating opportunities. CIAT Africa Highlight March No 9. pp. 1–2.

Biemans, W. G. (1991). User and third-party involvement in developing medical equipment innovations. *Technovation*, 11(3), 163–182.

Binz, H., and Reichle, M. (2005). Evaluation method to determine the success potential and the degree of innovation of technical product ideas and products, in A. Samuel and W. Lewis (eds.), *15th International Conference on Engineering Design: Engineering Design and the Global Economy ICED'05*. Melbourne (Australia), Institution of Engineers Australia/The Design Society, 222–236.

Birchall, D., and Tovstiga, G. (2005). *Capabilities for Strategic Advantage: Leading through Technological Innovation*. New York: Springer. .

Björk, J., and Magnusson, M. (2009). Where do good innovation ideas come from? Exploring the influence of network connectivity on innovation idea quality. *Journal of Product Innovation Management*, 26(6), 662–670.

Böhmer, A. I., and Lindemann, U. (2015). Open innovation ecosystem: Towards collaborative innovation. In *DS 80–8 Proceedings of the 20th International Conference on Engineering Design (ICED 15) Vol 8: Innovation and Creativity*, Milan, Italy, 27–30.07. 15 (pp. 031–040).

Breschi, S. (2008). Innovation-specific agglomeration economies and the spatial clustering of innovative firms, in C. Karlsson (ed.), *Handbook of Research on Innovation and Clusters*. Cheltenham: Edward Elgar, 167–192.

Breschi, S., Lissoni, F., and Montobbio, F. (2005). The geography of knowledge spillovers: Conceptual issues and measurement problems, in S. Breschi and F. Malerba (eds.), *Clusters, Networks, and Innovation*. Oxford: Oxford University Press, 343–376.

Breznitz, D. (2007). Innovation and the State: Political Choice and Strategies for Growth in Israel, Taiwan, and Ireland. London: Yale University Press.

Brown, J. S. (1998). Seeing differently: A role for pioneering research. *Research Technology Management*, 41(3), 24–33.

Brown, J. S., and Duguid, P. (1991). Organizational learning and communities-of-practice: Toward a unified view of working, learning, and innovation. *Organization Science*, 2(1), 40–57.

Bustinza, O. F., Gomes, E., Vendrell-Herrero, F., and Baines, T. (2019). Product-service innovation and performance: The role of collaborative partnerships and R&D intensity. *R&D Management*, 49(1), 33–45.

Callon, M., Lascoumes, P., and Barthe, Y. (2009). *Acting in an Uncertain World*. Cambridge, MA: MIT Press.

Cantwell, J. (2005). Innovation and competitiveness, in J. Fagerberg, D. C. Mowery and R. R. Nelson (eds.), The Oxford handbook of innovation. Oxford: Oxford University Press, 541–567.

Caputo, A. C., Cucchiella, F., Fratocchi, L., Pelagagge, P. M., and Scacchia, F. (2002). A methodological framework for innovation transfer to SMEs. *Industrial Management & Data Systems*, 102(5), 271–283.

Carlson, C. R., and Wilmot, W. W. (2006). Innovation: The five disciplines for creating what customers want. New York: Crown Business.

Chen, C. C. & Greene, P. G. & Crick, A. (1998). Does entrepreneurial self-efficacy distinguish entrepreneurs from managers?. *Journal of Business Venturing*, 13(4), 295–316

Central Bureau Statistics (2012). Innovation in the business sector 2006–2008. Commissioned by the National Council for Research and Development *(MOLP-MOP) and the ministry of industry, Trade and Labor.* Available at www.cbs.gov.il/publications12/1463innovation0608/pdf/introh/pdf/ (Hebrew).

Chandy, R. K., and Tellis, G. J. (1998). Organizing for radical product innovation: The overlooked role of willingness to cannibalize. *Journal of Marketing Research*, 35(4), 474–487.

Chesbrough, H. (2003a). Managing your false negatives. *Harvard Management Update*, 8(8), 8–9.

Chesbrough, H. (2003b). *Open Innovation: The New Imperative for Creating and Profiting from Technology.* Massachusetts: Harvard Business School Press.

Chesbrough, H. (2006). *Open Innovation Models: How to Thrive in the New Innovation Landscape.* Boston, MA: Harvard Business School Press.

Christensen, C. (1997). *The Innovator's Dilemma: When New Technologies Cause Great Firms to Fail.* Cambridge, MA: Harvard Business Review Press, 288p.

Christensen, C. M., Ojomo, E., and Van Bever, D. (2017). Africa's new generation of innovators. *Harvard Business Review*, 95(1), 129–136.

Church, C., and Elster, J. (2002). *Thinking Locally, Acting Nationally: Lessons for Policy from Local Action on Sustainable Development.* York: Joseph Rowntree Foundation.

Contractor, F. J. (2000). Valuing knowledge and intangible assets: Some general principles. *Knowledge and Process Management*, 7(4), 242–255.

Cooke, P. (2001). Regional innovation systems, clusters, and the knowledge economy. *Industrial and Corporate Change*, 10(4), 945–974, Cooke, 2001, p. 948.

Cooke, P. (2005). Regional knowledge capabilities and open innovation: Regional innovation systems and clusters in the asymmetric knowledge economy, in 254 References S. Breschi and F. Malerba (eds.), *Clusters, Networks, and Innovation.* Oxford: Oxford University Press, 80–110.

Cooper, R. G. (2005). *Product Leadership: Pathways to Profitable Innovation,* 2nd éd. New York: Basic Books.

Corsaro, D., Cantù, C., and Tunisini, A. (2012). Actors' heterogeneity in innovation networks. *Industrial Marketing Management*, 41(5), 780–789.

Corsaro, D., Ramos, C., Henneberg, S. C., & Naudé, P. (2012). The impact of network configurations on value constellations in business markets—The case of an innovation network. *Industrial Marketing Management*, 41(1), 54–67.

Coulson-Thomas, C. (2012). *Talent Management 2.* Peterborough: Policy Publications.

Coulson-Thomas, C. (2017). Stimulating creativity, enabling innovation and supporting entrepreneurship. *Management Services*, 2017(Summer), 26–29.

Cravens, D. W., Piercy, N. F., and Low, G. S. (2002). The innovation challenges of proactive cannabalisation and discontinuous technology. *European Business Review*, 14(4), 257–267.

Cumbers, A., MacKinnon, D., and Chapman, K. (2008). Innovation, collaboration and learning in regional clusters: A study of SMEs in the Aberdeen Oil Complex, in C. Karlsson (ed.), *Handbook of Research on Innovation and Clusters*. Cheltenham: Edward Elgar, 300–317.

Damanpour, F. (1991). Organizational innovation: A meta-analysis of effects of determinants and moderators. *Academy of Management Journal*, 34(3), 555–590.

Daniels, C. U. (2014). Policy support for innovation at grassroots in developing countries: Perspectives from Nigeria. *Journal of Science, Technology and Society*, 1–17.

De Beule, F., Van Den Bulcke, D., & Zhang, H. (2008). 13 The reciprocal relationship between transnationals and clusters: a literature review. *Handbook of Research on Cluster Theory*, 1, 219.

De Beule, F., Van Den Bulcke, D., and Zhang, H. (2008). The reciprocal relationship between transnationals and clusters: A literature review, in C. Karlsson (ed.), *Handbook of Research on Cluster Theory*. Cheltenham: Edward Elgar.

De Meyer, A., Nakane, J., Miller, J. G., and Ferdows, K. (1989). Flexibility: The next competitive battle. *Strategic Management Journal*, 10(2), 135–144.

Deborah, J. J. (2011). What is an innovation Ecosystem. By National Science Foundation, Arlington. [online] Available at: http://ercassoc.org/sites/default/files/topics/policy_studies/DJackson_Innovation%20Ecosystem_03-15-11.pdf.

Delgado, M., Porter, M. E., and Stern, S. (2010). Clusters and entrepreneurship. *Journal of Economic Geography*, 10(4), 495–518.

Dillon, T. A., Lee, R. K., and Matheson, D. (2005). Value innovation: Passport to wealth creation. *Research-Technology Management*, 48(2), 22–36.

Doloreux, D. (2004). Regional networks of small and medium sized enterprises: Evidence from the metropolitan area of Ottawa in Canada. *European Planning Studies*, 12(2), 173–189.

Doyle, P. (2000). Value-based marketing. *Journal of Strategic Marketing*, 8(4), 299–311.

Drucker, P. F. (1988). The coming of the new organization. *Harvard Business Review*, 45–53.

Du, J., Love, J. H., and Roper, S. (2007). The innovation decision: An economic analysis. *Technovation*, 27(12), 766–773.

Dunning, J. H. (1998). Location and the multinational enterprise: A neglected factor?. *Journal of International Business Studies*, 29(1), 45–66.

Dunning, J. H., and Lundan, S. M. (2008). *Multinational Enterprises and the Global Economy*. Chellenham: Edward Elgar Publishing.

Edquist, C. (ed.). (1997). *Systems of Innovation: Technologies, Institutions, and Organizations*. London: Psychology Press.

Edquist, C., and Hommen, L. (1999). Systems of innovation: Theory and policy for the demand side. *Technology in Society*, 21(1), 63–79.

Ellonen, R., Blomqvist, K., and Puumalainen, K. (2008). The role of trust in organisational innovativeness. *European Journal of Innovation Management*. 11(2), 160–181.

Esteve-Pérez, S., and Mañez-Castillejo, J. A. (2008). The resource-based theory of the firm and firm survival. *Small Business Economics*, 30(3), 231–249.

Estrin, J. (2009). *Closing the Innovation Gap. Reigniting the Spark of Creativity in a Global Economy*. McGraw Hill: San Francisco.

Eversheim, W. (2003). *Innovations management Fu"r Technische Produkte*. Berlin: Springer.

Eyal-Cohen, M. (2019). Innovation agents. *Washington & Lee Law Review*, 76, 163.

Fagerberg, J. (2005). Innovation, a guide to the literature, in J. Fagerberg, D. C. Mowery and R. R. Nelson (eds.), *The Oxford Handbook of Innovation*. Oxford: Oxford University Press, 1–26.

Feldman, M. P. (1994). *The Geography of Innovation*. Dordrecht: Kluwer Academic Publishers.

Feldman, M. P. (2008). The entrepreneurial event revisited: Firm formation in a regional context, in C. Karlsson (ed.), *Handbook of research on Innovation and Clusters*. Cheltenham: Edward Elgar, 318–342.

Fingleton, B., Igliori, D., and Moore, B. (2008). Employment growth in ICT clusters: New evidence from Great Britain, in C. Karlsson (ed.), *Handbook of Research on Innovation and Clusters*. Cheltenham: Edward Elgar, 79–106.

Freeman, C., and L. Soete (1985). *Information Technology and Employment: An Assessment*. Brighton: Science Policy Research Unit, University of Sussex.

Galizzi, G., and Venturini, L. (1996). Product innovation in the food industry: Nature, characteristics and determinants. In G. Galizzi and L. Venturini (eds.), *Economics of Innovation: The Case of Food Industry*. Heidelberg: Physica-Verlag, 133–153.

Gassmann, O., and Keupp, M. M. (2007). The competitive advantage of early and rapidly internationalising SMEs in the biotechnology industry: A knowledge-based view. *Journal of World Business*, 42(3), 350–366.

Geels, F., and Raven, R. (2006). Non-linearity and expectations in niche-development trajectories: Ups and downs in Dutch biogas development (1973–2003). *Technology Analysis & Strategic Management*, 18(3–4), 375–392.

Gemser, G., and Wijnberg, N. M. (1995). Horizontal networks, appropriability conditions and industry life cycles. *Journal of Industry Studies*, 2(2), 129–140.

Gemünden, H. G., and Heydebreck, P. (1995). The influence of business strategies on technological network activities. *Research Policy*, 24(6), 831–849.

Gillier, T., Kazakci, A. O., and Piat, G. (2012). The generation of common purpose in innovation partnerships. *European Journal of Innovation Management*, 15(3), 372–392.

Gladwell, M. (2011). The tweaker. *The New Yorker*. http://www.newyorker. com/ reporting/2011/11/14/111114fa_fact_gladwell?currentPage=all.

Granovetter, M. (1985). Economic action and social structure: The problem of embeddedness. *American Journal of Sociology*, 91(3), 481–510.

Grant, R. M. (1991). The resource-based theory of competitive advantage: Implications for strategy formulation. *California Management Review*, 33(3), 114–135.

Gratton, L. (2006). Co-operation without frontiers. *Business Strategy Review*, 17(2), 65–67.

Grunert, K. G., Harmsen, H., Meulenberg, M. T. G., Kuiper, E., Ottowitz, T., Declerck, F., Traill, B., and Goransson, G. (1997). A framework for analysing innovation in the food industry. Boston, MA: Springer, 1–37.

Guan, J., and Chen, K. (2012). Modeling the relative efficiency of national innovation systems. *Research Policy*, 41(1), 102–115.

Gupta, A. K. (2013). Tapping the entrepreneurial potential of grassroots innovation. *Stanford Social Innovation Rev*iew, 11(3), 18–20.

Gupta, A. K., Sinha, R., Koradia, D., Patel, R., Parmar, M., Rohit, P., Patel, H., Patel, K., Chand, V. S., James, T. J., Chandan, A., Patel, M., Prakash, T. N., and Vivehanandan, P. (2003) Mobilizing grassroots' technological innovations and traditional knowledge, values and institutions: Articulating social and ethical capital, *Futures* 35(9), 975–987.

Hagedoorn, J. (2002). Inter-firm R&D partnerships: An overview of major trends and patterns since 1960. *Research Policy*, 31(4), 477–492.

Håkansson, H., and Snehota, I. (1989). No business is an island: the network concept of business strategy. *Scandinavian Journal of Management Studies*, 5(3), 187–200.

Håkansson, H. & J. Johanson (1992). A model of industrial networks. In B. Axelsson, B., & G. Easton (eds.), *Industrial Networks: A New View of Reality*. London: Routledge, 28–34.

Haldin-Herrgard, T. (2000). Difficulties in the diffusion of Tacit Knowledge in organizations. *Journal of Intellectual Capital*, 1(4): 357–365.

Hamel, G. (2003). Innovation as a deep capability. *Leader to Leader*, 27(Winter), 19–24.

Hamel, G., and Prahalad, C. K. (1994). Competing for the future. *Harvard Business Review*, 72(4), 122–128.

Hansen, C. T., and Andreasen, M. M. (2006). Conceiving product ideas in an initial and uncertain design situation, in NordDesign Conference, Reykjavik, August 16–18, 32–41.

Hansen, M. T., and Birkinshaw, J. (2007). The innovation value chain. *Harvard Business Review*, 85(6), 121.

Hansen, M. T., Nohria, N., and Tierney, T. (1999). What's your strategy for managing knowledge. *The Knowledge Management Yearbook 2000–2001*, 77(2), 106–116.

Harel, R., Schwartz, D., and Kaufmann, D. (2019). Small businesses are promoting innovation!! Do we know this?. *Small Enterprise Research*, 26(1), 18–35.

Harless, J. H. (1986). Guiding performance with job aids. *Introduction to Performance Technology*, 1, 106–124.

Harper, S. M., and Becker, S. W. (2004). On the leading edge of innovation: a comparative study of innovation practices. *Southern Business Review*, 29(2), 1.

Harrison, D., and Waluszewski, A. (2008). The development of a user network as a way to re-launch an unwanted product. *Research Policy*, 37(1), 115–130.

Hart, S. L. (1995). A natural-resource-based view of the firm. *The Academy of Management Review*, 20(4), 986–1014.

Helfat, C. E., Finkelstein, S., Mitchell, W., Peteraf, M., Singh, H., Teece, D., and Winter, S. G. (2007). *Dynamic Capabilities: Understanding Strategic Change in Organizations*. Hoboken, NJ: John Wiley & Sons.

Hertner, P., and Jones, G. (1986). *Multinationals–Theory and History*. Gower Publishing Company, Limited. Aldershot: Gower

Hewitt-Dundas, N. (2006). Resource and capability constraints to innovation in small and large plants. *Small Business Economics*, 26(3), 257–277.

Hippel, E. V. (2005). *The Sources of Innovation*. New York: Oxford University Press

Hoerl, R.W. and Gardner, M. (2010). Lean Six Sigma, creativity, and innovation. *International Journal of Lean Six Sigma,* 1(1), 30–38.

Hoffman, K., Parejo, M., Bessant, J., and Perren, L. (1998). Small firms, R&D, technology and innovation in the UK: A literature review. *Technovation*, 18(1), 39–55. doi:10.1016/S0166-4972(97)00102-8.

Hopkins, R., and Lipman, P. (2009). *Who We Are and What We Do*. Totnes: Transition Network.

Howells, J. (2002). Tacit knowledge, innovation and economic geography. *Urban Studies*, 39(5–6), 871–884.

Huber, D., Kaufmann, H., and Steinmann, M. (2017). *Bridging the Innovation Gap: Blueprint for the Innovative Enterprise* New York City: Springer.

Inkpen, A. C. (1996). Creating knowledge through collaboration. *California Management Review*, 39(1), 123–140.

Isaksen, A. (2008). The clustering of software consultancy in Oslo: Reason for and effects of clustering, in C. Karlsson (ed.), *Handbook of Research on Innovation and Clusters*. Cheltenham: Edward Elgar, 193–207.

Israeli Innovation Authority (2018). Israeli innovations breakthrough products that changed the world Ministry of Economy and Industry. Retrieved http//innovationisrael.mag.calltext.co.il/magazine/80.

Jacobs, H., and Zulu, C. (2012). Reaping the benefits of value innovation: Lessons for small agribusinesses in Africa. *African Journal of Business Management*, 6(33), 9510–9523.

Jansen, J., Van Den Bosch, F., Volbera, H. (2006). Exploratory innovation, exploitative innovation and performance: Effects of organizational antecedents and environmental moderators. *Management Science* 52(11), 1661–1674.

Jay, K., and Ria, D. (1999). Competitive advantage through anticipation, innovation and relationships. *Management Decision*, 37(1), 51–56.

Joe, T., Bessant, J., and Pavitt, K. (2005). *Managing Innovation: Integrating Technological, Market and Organizational Change*. Hoboken, NJ: John Wiley & Sons.

Johannessen, J. A., Olsen, B., and Lumpkin, G. T. (2001). Innovation as newness: What is new, how new, and new to whom?. *European Journal of Innovation Management*, 4(1), 20–31.

Johannessen, J-A., Olaisen, J., and Olsen, B. (1999). Managing and organizing innovation in the knowledge economy. *European Journal of Innovation Management*, 2(3), 116–128.

Johansson, F. (2004). *The Medici Effect: Breakthrough Insights at the Intersection of Ideas, Concepts, and Cultures*. Boston, MA: Harvard Business School Press.

Johnson, M. D., and Kirchain, R. E. (2011). The importance of product development cycle time and cost in the development of product families. *Journal of Engineering Design*, 22(2), 87–112.

Juma, C. (2011). *The New Harvest: Agriculture Innovation in Africa*. New York: Oxford University Press. Oxford.

Kaaria, S., Sanginga, P., Njuki, J., Delve, R., Chitsike, C., and Best, R. (2009). Enabling rural innovation in Africa: An approach for empowering smallholder farmers to access market opportunities for improved livelihoods. Paper prepared for the conference "farmer first revisited: farmer participatory research and development twenty years on", Institute of Development Studies, University of Sussex, UK, 12–14 December 2007.

Kalua, F. A., Awotedu, A., Kamwanja, L. A., and Saka, J. D. K. (2009). Science, technology and innovation for public health in Africa. *Monograph*. NEPAD Office of Science and Technology, Pretoria, Republic of South Africa.

Kandampully, J. (1996). Quality the uncompromising core element in services: in Asia Pacific Tourism Association 96 Conference Proceedings, Townsville.

Kandampully, J. (2002). Innovation as the core competency of a service organisation: The role of technology, knowledge and networks. *European Journal of Innovation Management*, 5(1), 18–26.

Kaplan, R. S., and Norton, D. P. (2004). Measuring the strategic readiness of intangible assets. *Harvard Business Review*, 82(2), 52–63.

Karlsson, A., and Törlind, P. (2013). What happens to rejected ideas?– Exploring the life of ideas following the completion of projects. In DS 75-3: Proceedings of the 19th International Conference on Engineering Design (ICED13) Design For Harmonies, Vol. 3: Design Organization and Management, Seoul, August 19–22, 229–238.

Keizer, J. A., and Halman, J. I. (2007). Diagnosing risk in radical innovation projects. *Research-Technology Management*, 50(5), 30–36.

Ketels, C. H. M. (2008). Microeconomic determinants of location competitiveness for MNEs, in J. H. Dunning and P. Gugler (eds.), *Foreign Direct Investment, Location and Competitiveness*. Oxford: Elsevier, 111–131.

Kiely, T. (1993). The idea makers. *Technology Review*, 96(1), 32.

Kim, W. C., and Mauborgne, R. (1997). Value innovation. *Harvard Business Review*, 75(1): 102–112.

Kim, W. C., and Mauborgne, R. (2005). Value innovation: A leap into the blue ocean. *Journal of Business Strategy*, 26, 22–28.

Kirner, E., SpomenkaMaloca, Rogowski, T., Slama, A., Oliver Som, Spitzley, A., and Wagner, K. (2007) KritischeErfolgsfaktorenzurSteigerung der Innovationsfähigkeit, Karlsruhe: FraunhoferInstitutfürArbeitswirtschaft und Organisation IAO und Universität Stuttgart (InstitutfürArbeitswissenschaftundTechnologiemanagement).

Kline, S. J., and Rosenberg, N. (1986). An overview of innovation, in R. Landou and N. Rosenberg, (eds) *The Positive Sum Strategy*. Washington, DC: National Academy Press.

Koellinger, P. (2008). Why are some entrepreneurs more innovative than others?. *Small Business Economics*, 31(1), 21.

Koestler, A. (1989). *The Art of Creation*. London: Arkana.

Kogut, B., and Zander, U. (1992). Knowledge of the firm, combinative capabilities, and the replication of technology. *Organization Science*, 3(3), 383–397.

Kohtala, C. (2016). Making sustainability: How Fab Labs address environmental issues', doctoral dissertation, Helsinki: Aalto University.

Kooskora, M. (2004). Innovation and knowledge sharing – Essentiality in Today's Business World. EBS Review.

Kotler, F., and Keller, K. (2008). *Marketing Menedzhment [Marketing Management]*. Saint-Petersburg: Piter.

Kraemer-Mbula, E., and SonsWamae, W. (2010). The relevance of innovation systems to developing countries, in E. Kraemer-Mbula and W. Wamae (eds.), *Innovation and the Development Agenda*, Paris: OECD/IDRC, 39–65.

Krugman, P. (1994). Competitiveness: A dangerous obsession. *Foreign Affairs*, 73, 28.

Lavado, A. C., and Cabrera, R. V. (2008). Managing functional diversity, risk taking and incentives for teams to achieve radical innovations. *R&D Management*, 38(1), 35–50.

Lawson, B., and Samson, D. (2001). Developing innovation capability in organisations: A dynamic capabilities approach. *International Journal of Innovation Management*, 5(03), 377–400.

Lazonick, W. (2005). The innovative firm, in Fagerberg J, D. Mowery and R. R. Nelson (eds.), *The Oxford Handbook of Innovation*. New York: Oxford University Press, 29–55.

Lee, K., Juma, C., and Mathews, J. (2014). Innovation capabilities for sustainable development in Africa. UNU-WIDER Working Paper 062.

Leifer, R. (2001). Richard Leifer on radical innovation. *Ubiquity*, 2001(February), 2.

Leiponen, A., and Helfat, C. E. (2010). Innovation objectives, knowledge sources, and the benefits of breadth. *Strategic Management Journal*, 31(2), 224–236.

Leonard-Barton, D. (1992). Core capabilities and core rigidities: A paradox in managing new product development. *Strategic Management Journal*, 13(S1), 111–125.

Lev, B. (2001). *Intangibles, Management, and Reporting*. Washington, MA: The Brookings Institution.

Levidow, L. (1998). Democratizing technology - or technologizing democracy? Regulating agricultural biotechnology in Europe. *Technology in Society*, 20(2), 211–226.

Lindsay, J., Perkins, C. A., and Karanjikar, M. (2009). *Conquering Innovation Fatigue: Overcoming the Barriers to Personal and Corporate Success*. Hoboken, NJ: John Wiley & Sons.

Lundvall, B.-A. (1992). *National System of Innovation: Toward a Theory of Innovation and Interactive Learning*. London: Pinter Publishers.

Luoma-aho, V., and Halonen, S. (2010). Intangibles and innovation: The role of communication in the innovation ecosystem. *Innovation Journalism*, 7(2), 1–20.

MacKenzi, G. (1998). *Orbiting the Giant Hairball*. New York: Viking.

Madrid-Guijarro, A., Garcia, D., and Van Auken, H. (2009). Barriers to innovation among Spanish manufacturing SMEs. *Journal of Small Business Management*, 47(4), 465–488.

Mahagaonkar, P. (2008). *Corruption and Innovation: A Grease or Sand Relationship*. Jena: Jena Economic Research Papers, No. 2008, 017.

Makadok, R. (2001). Toward a synthesis of the resource-based and dynamic-capability views of rent creation. *Strategic Management Journal*, 22(5), 387–401.

Malik, T. H. (2013). National institutional differences and cross-border university-industry knowledge transfer. *Research Policy*, 42(3), 776–787.

Malmelin, N. (200 7). Communication Capital. Modeling Corporate Communications as an organizational asset. *Corporate Communication as an International Journal*, 12(3), 298–310.

Marques, C. S., and Ferreira, J. (2009). SME innovative capacity, competitive advantage and performance in a 'traditional' industrial region of Portugal. *Journal of Technology Management & Innovation*, 4(4), 53–68.

Martín-de Castro, G., Delgado-Verde, M., Navas-López, J. E., and Cruz-González, J. (2013). The moderating role of innovation culture in the relationship between knowledge assets and product innovation. *Technological Forecasting and Social Change*, 80(2), 351–363.

Maskell, P., and Malmberg, A. (1999). Localized learning and industrial competitiveness. *Cambridge Journal of Economics*, 23, 167–186.

Mast, C., Huck, S., and Zerfas, A. (2005). Innovation Communication, Outline of the concept and Empirical finding for Germany. *Innovation Journalism*, 2(4), 165–179.

Mathews, J. A. (2013). The renewable energies technology surge: A new techno-economic paradigm in the making?'. *Futures*, 46, 10–22.

Mazzucato, M. (2011). *The Entrepreneurial State*. London: Demos.

McCormick, D., and Maalu, J. (2011). Innovation hubs and small and medium enterprises in Africa: Setting the policy agenda. *Mimeo Institute for Development Studies and the University of Nairobi*. Retrieved from http://www.uonbi.ac.ke/faculties/ids/index.html.

McLaughlin, G., and Caraballo, V. (2013). *Chance or Choice: Unlocking Innovation Success*. Boca Raton, FL: Taylor and Francis.

Meigounpoory, M. R., Rezvani, M., and Afshar, M. (2015). Identification of service innovation dimensions in service organizations. *International Journal of Management, Accounting and Economics*, 2(7), 737–748.

Metcalfe, J. S. (2005). Systems failure and the case for innovation policy, in P. Llerena, M. Matt, and A. Avadikyan (eds.), *Innovation Policy in a Knowledge-based Economy: Theory and Practice*. Germany: Springer, 47–74.

Metcalfe, S., and Ramlogan, R. (2008). Innovation systems and the competitive process in developing economies. *The Quarterly Review of Economics and Finance*, 48(2), 433–446.

Meyer, M. M. (2013). *The Innovator's Path: How Individuals, Teams, and Organizations Can Make Innovation Business-as-Usual*. Hoboken, NJ: John Wiley & Sons.

Miron, J. R. (2010). *The Geography of Competition*. Berlin: Springer Science + Business Media, LLC.

Moenaert, R. K., Caeldries, F., Lievens, A., and Wauters, E. (2000). Communication flows in international product innovation teams. *Journal of Product Innovation Management: An International Publication of the Product Development & Management Association*, 17(5), 360–377.

Moore, K., and Lewis, D. (1999). *Birth of the Multinational: 2000 Years of Ancient Business History, from Ashur to Augustus*. Copahengen: Handelshojskolens Forlag.

Mudambi, R., and Swift, T. (2012). Multinational enterprises and the geographical clustering of innovation. *Industry and Innovation*, 19(1), 1–21.

Myers, R., and Assink, M. (2006). Inhibitors of disruptive innovation capability: A conceptual model. *European Journal of Innovation Management*.

Nakamura, J., and Mihaly, C. (2002). The motivational sources of creativity as viewed from the paradigm of positive psychology, in L. G. Aspinwall and U. M. Staudinger's *A Psychology of Human Strengths: Fundamental Questions and Future Directions for a Positive Psychology*. Washington, DC: American Psychology Association, November 2002.

Nelson, R. (1993). *National Innovation Systems: A Comparative Analysis*. New York: Oxford University Press.

Nelson, R. R., and Winter, S. G. (1977). In search of a useful theory of innovation. *Research Policy*, 6, 36.

Niosi, J. (2003). Alliances are not enough explaining rapid growth in biotechnology firms. *Research Policy*, 32(5), 737–750.

Nissen, H. A., Evald, M. R., and Clarke, A. H. (2014). Knowledge sharing in heterogeneous teams through collaboration and cooperation: Exemplified through Public–Private-Innovation partnerships. *Industrial Marketing Management*, 43(3), 473–482.

Nonaka, I. (1991). The knowledge-creating company. *Harvard Business Review*, 69(6), 96–104.

Öberg, C., and Shih, T. T. Y. (2014). Divergent and convergent logic of firms: Barriers and enablers for development and commercialization of innovations. *Industrial Marketing Management*, 43(3), 419–428.

OECD (2005). The measurement of scientific and technological activities. *Guidelines for Collecting and Interpreting Innovation Data: Oslo Manual* (3rd ed.). Paris: OECD Publishing.

OECD (2010). *The OECD Innovation Strategy: Getting a Head Start on Tomorrow*. Paris: OECD.

OECD (2013). *Perspectives on Global Development 2013: Industrial Policies in a Changing World*. Paris: OECD Publishing.

OECD (2015). *Innovation Policies for Inclusive Development: Scaling Up Inclusive Innovations*. Paris: Organisation for Economic Cooperation and Development World Bank (2012). *Inclusive Green Growth: The Pathway to a Sustainable World*. Washington, DC: World.

Ojeaga (2016). Can Africa's young drive innovation? Investigating the effect of entrepreneurial innovation on economic growth in Africa. *Journal of Applied Quantitative Methods*, 10(4), 15–36.

Oluwatobi, S., Efobi, U., Olurinola, I., and Alege, P. (2015). Innovation in Africa: Why institutions matter. *South African Journal of Economics*, 83(3), 390–410.

Onyeiwu, S. (2015). Does lack of innovation and absorptive capacity retard economic growth in Africa? In *Growth and institutions in African Development*. Routledge, 63–80.

O'Sullivan, D., and Dooley, L. (2008). *Applying Innovation*. Newbury Park, CA: Sage publications.

Owens, T., and Fernandez, O. (2014). *The Lean Enterprise: How Corporations can Innovate like Startups*. Hoboken, NJ: John Wiley & Sons.

Oyelaran-Oyeyinka, B., Laditan, G. O. A., and Esubiyi, A. O. (1996). Industrial innovation in Sub-Saharan Africa: The manufacturing sector in Nigeria. *Research Policy*, 25(7), 1081–1096.

Pavitt, K. (2005). Innovation processes, in J. Fagerberg, D. C. Mowery and R. R. Nelson (eds.), *The Oxford Handbook of Innovation*, New York: Oxford University Press, 86–114.

Peppers, D., and Rogers, M. (1997). The $15,000 rug. *Marketing Tools*, 4–6.

Perez, C., and Soete, L. (1988). Catching-up in technology: Entry barriers and windows of opportunity, in Dosi et al. (eds.), *Technical Change and Economic Theory*. London: Pinter Publishers, 458–479.

Perks, H., and Moxey, S. (2011). Market-facing innovation networks: How lead firms partition tasks, share resources and develop capabilities. *Industrial Marketing Management*, 40(8), 1224–1237.

Peters, T. (1997).*Thriving on Chaos*. London: Pan Books.

Pianta M. (2003). Innovation and employment, in I. Fagerberg, D. Mowery and R. R. Nelson (eds.), *Handbook of Innovation*. Oxford: Oxford University Press.

Piatier, A. (1984). *Barriers to Innovation*. London; Dover, NH: F. Pinter.

Pine, B. J. (1991). *Paradigm shift: from mass production to mass customization.* Doctoral dissertation, Massachusetts Institute of Technology.

Polenske, K. R. (2004). Competition, collaboration and cooperation: An uneasy triangle in networks of firms and regions. *Regional Studies*, 38(9), 1029–1043.

Porter, M. E. (1996). Competitive advantage, agglomeration economies, and regional policy. *International Regional Science Review*, 19(1–2), 85–90.

Porter, M. E. (1998). Clusters and the new economics of competition, *Harvard Business Review*, 76(6), 77–90.

Porter, M. E. (2000). Location, competition and economic development: Local clusters in a global economy. *Economic Development Quarterly*, 14(1), 15–34.

Porter, M. E., and Stern, S. (2001). Innovation: Location matters. *MIT Sloan Management Review*, 42(4), 28.Powell, W (1998). Learning from Collaboration: Knowledge and Networks in the Biotechnology and pharmaceutical industries. *California Management Review*, 40(3), 228–240.

Powell, W., and Brantley, P. (1992). Competitive cooperation in biotechnology: Learning through networks? In N. Nohria & R.G. Eccles (eds.), *Networks and Organizations: Structure, Form, and Action*. Boston, MA: Harvard Business School Press, 365–394.

Powell, W. W., Koput, K. W., and Smith-Doerr, L. (1996). Interorganizational collaboration and the locus of innovation: Networks of learning in biotechnology. *Administrative Science Quarterly*, 41, 116–145.

Prahalad, C. K. (1993). The role of core competencies in the corporation. *Research-Technology Management*, 36(6), 40–47.

Prahalad, C. K., and Ramaswamy, V. (2004). Co-creation experiences: The next practice of value creation. *Journal of Interactive Marketing*, 18(3), 5–14.

Qiu, L., Han, Q., and Jiang, J., (2019). Promoting high-quality development of innovation and entrepreneurship. 2 (2), 26–39.

Rampersad, G., Quester, P., and Troshani, I. (2010). Managing innovation networks: Exploratory evidence from ICT, biotechnology and nanotechnology networks. *Industrial Marketing Management*, 39(5), 793–805.

Rees, K. (2005). Interregional collaboration and innovation in Vancouver's emerging high-tech cluster. *Tijdschrift voor Economische en Sociale Geografie* 96(3), 298–312.

Reypens, C., Lievens, A., and Blazevic, V. (2016). Leveraging value in multi-stakeholder innovation networks: A process framework for value co-creation and capture. *Industrial Marketing Management*, 56, 40–50.

Rhee, J., Park, T., and Lee, D. H. (2010). Drivers of innovativeness and performance for innovative SMEs in South Korea: Mediation of learning orientation. *Technovation*, 30(1), 65–75.

Richards, L. G. (1998). Stimulating creativity: Teaching engineers to be innovators. In FIE'98. 28th Annual Frontiers in Education Conference. Moving from 'Teacher-Centered' to 'Learner-Centered' Education. Conference Proceedings (Cat. No. 98CH36214), (Vol. 3, 1034–1039). IEEE.

Robotham, A. J., and Guldbrandsen, M. (2000). What is the new paradigm in product quality?. Proceedings NordDesign, 2000, DTU, Lyngby, Denmark. Romer, P. M., 1986. Increasing returns and long-run growth. *Journal of Political Economy*, 94(5), 1002–1037.

Romero, I., and Martínez-Román, J. A. (2012). Self-employment and innovation. Exploring the determinants of innovative behavior in small businesses. *Research Policy*, 41(1), 178–189.

Roper, S., Dub, J., Love, J. H. (2008). Modelling the innovation value chain. *Research Policy*, 37(6/7), 961–977.

Roper, S., and Xia, H. (2014). Innovation, innovation strategy and survival. ERC Research Paper, 17.

Rothwell, R. (1994). Towards the fifth-generation innovation process. *International Marketing Review*, 11(1), 7–31.

Ruppel, C. P., and Harrington, S. J. (2000). The relationship of communication, ethical work climate, and trust to commitment and innovation. *Journal of Business Ethics*, 25(4), 313–328.

Schipper, T., and Swets, M. (2012). *Innovative Lean Development: How to Create, Implement and Maintain a Learning Culture Using Fast Learning Cycles*. Florida: CRC Press.

Schonberger, R. J. (1987). Frugal manufacturing. *Harvard Business Review*, 65(5), 95–100.

Schumpeter, J. A. (1934). The theory of economic development, translated by Redvers Opie. *Harvard: Economic Studies*, 46, 1600-0404.

Schumpeter, J. A. (1939). *Business Cycles: A Theoretical, Historical, and Statistical Analysis of the Capitalist Process*. New York City: McGraw Hill.

Schumpeter, J. A. (1950). *Capitalism, Socialism, and Democracy... With a New Preface.*. George Allen & Unwin.

Schumpeter, J. A (1980). *The Theory of Economic Development*. England Translation

Scott, A. J. (2006). Entrepreneurship, innovation and industrial development: Geography and the creative field revisited. *Small Business Economics*, 26(1), 1–24.

Senge, P. (2007). *Pátá disciplína – Teorie a praxe učíci se organizace*. Praha: Management Press.

Seyfang, G., and Haxeltine, A. (2012). Growing grassroots innovations: Exploring the role of community-based initiatives in governing sustainable energy transitions. *Environment and Policy C. Government and Policy*, 30(3), 381–400.

Seyfang, G., and Smith, A. (2007). Grassroots innovations for sustainable development: Towards a new research and policy agenda. *Environmental Politics*, 16(4), 584–603.

Shapiro, S. M. (2002). 24/7 *Innovation: A Blueprint for Surviving and Thriving in an Age of Change*. New York City: McGraw-Hill.

Sieg, J. H., Wallin, M. W., and Von Krogh, G. (2010). Managerial challenges in open innovation: A study of innovation intermediation in the chemical industry. *R&D Management*, 40(3), 281–291.

Simmie, J. (2008). The contribution of clustering to innovation: From Porter I agglomeration to Porter II export base theories, in C. Karlsson(ed.), *Handbook of Research on Innovation and Clusters: Cases and Policies*, Cheltenham: Edward Elgar, 19–32.

Simon, H. A. (1947). *Administrative Behavior*. New York: Macmillan.

Singularity, U. (2014). An Overview for the Kansas City Chamber of Commerce, [online], Available at http://www.kcchamber.com/KCChamber/media/Media/PDFs/2014LeadershipExchange/SingularityUniverstiy-ExponentialLearning.pdf [accessed: 01.12.2014].

Smith, A., Hielscher, S., Dickel, S., Söderberg, J., and van Oost, E. (2013) Grassroots digital fabrication and makerspaces: Reconfiguring, relocating and recalibrating innovation?, SPRU Working Paper Series SWPS 2013-02, Brighton: University of Sussex.

Smith, A., and Stirling, A. (2016). Grassroots innovation & innovation democracy. Working Paper, STEPS Centre, University of Sussex, Brighton.

Spender, J. C. (1996). Making knowledge the basis of a dynamic theory of the firm. *Strategic Management Journal*, 17(S2), 45–62.

Steiner, G. (2006). The planetary model as an organizational framework for the generation of innovation: A critical reflection on today's innovation practice. *Our Economy* (*Nase Gospodarstvo*), 51(1–2), 18–23

Sundbo, J., and Gallouj, F. (2000). Innovation as a loosely coupled system in services. *International Journal of Services Technology and Management*, 1(1), 15–3.

Tan, A. R., and McAloone, T. C. (2006). Understanding and developing innovative products and services: The essential elements. In *DS 36: Proceedings DESIGN 2006, the 9th International Design Conference, Dubrovnik, Croatia*.

Teece, D. J., Pisano, G., and Shuen, A. (1997). Dynamic capabilities and strategic management. *Strategic Management Journal*, 18(7), 509–533.

Tidd, J., and Bessant, J. (2009). *Managing Innovation: Integrating Technological, Market and Organizational Change*. Fourth Edition, Chichester: Hoboken, NJ: John Wiley & Sons Ltd..

Tidd, J., Bessant, J., and Pavitt, K. (2002). Learning through alliances, in J. Henry and D. Mayle (eds.), *Managing Innovation and Change*, 2nd ed., London: Sage, 167–188.

Tinguely, X. (2013). *The New Geography of Innovation: Clusters, Competitiveness and Theory*. New York: Springer.

Torrance, E. P. (1972). Creative young women in today's world. *Exceptional Children*, 38(8), 597–603.

Tseng, M. M., and Piller, F. T. (2003). The customer centric enterprise, in *The Customer Centric Enterprise*. New York: Springer, 3–16.

Tsoukas, H. (1996). The firm as a distributed knowledge system: A constructionist approach. *Strategic Management Journal*, 17(S2), 11–25.

Tulus, T., and Hamonangan, T. (2011). Development of small and medium enterprises in a developing country. *Journal of Enterprising Communities*, 5, 68–82.

Tushman, M., and Nadler, D. (1986). Organizing for innovation. *California Management Review*, 28(3), 74–92.

Urbancova, H. (2013). Competitive advantage achievement through innovation and knowledge. *Journal of Competitiveness*, 5(1), 82–96

Usher, A. P. (1954). *A History of Mechanical Inventions*. Cambridge, MA: Harvard University Press.

Vahs, D., and Brem, A. (2013). *Innovationsmanagement: Von der Idee zur erfolgreichen Vermarktung (4. Ausg.)*. Stuttgart: Schäffer-Poeschel Verlag.

Van de Ven, A. H., Polley, D. E., Garud, R., and Venkataraman, S. (1999). *The Innovation Journey*. New York: Oxford University Press.

Van der Panne, G., Van Beers, C., and Kleinknecht, A. (2003). Success and failure of innovation: A literature review. *International Journal of Innovation Management*, 7(03), 309–338.

Vanhaverbeke, W., and Cloodt, M. (2006). Open innovation in value networks, in H. Chesbrough, W. Vanhaverbeke,, and J. West, (eds.), *Open innovation: Researching a new paradigm*. New York: Oxford University Press.

Varis and Littunen (2010). Types of innovation, sources of information and performance in entrepreneurial SMEs. *European Journal of Innovation Management*, 13(2), 128–134.

Veblen, T. (1899). *The Theory of the Leisure*. Class (New York: The New American Library, 1953).

Verloop, J., (2004). *Insight in Innovation: Managing Innovation by Understanding the Laws of Innovation*. Amsterdam: Elsevier Science.

Visnjic, I., Wiengarten, F., and Neely, A. (2016). Only the brave: Product innovation, service business model innovation, and their impact on performance. *Journal of Product Innovation Management*, 33(1), 36–52.

Vivarelli, M., Evangelista, R., and Pianta, M. (1996). Innovation and employment: Evidence from Italian manufacturing. *Research Policy* 25: 1013–1026.

Von Hippel, E. (1986). Lead users: A source of novel product concepts. *Management Science*, 32(7), 791–805.

Von Hippel, E. (1988). *The Source of Innovation*. Oxford: Oxford University Press.

Von Hippel, E. (2005). *Democratizing Innovation*. Cambridge, MA: MIT Press.

Wang, C. L., and Ahmed, P. K. (2004). The development and validation of the organisational innovativeness construct using confirmatory factor analysis. *European Journal of Innovation Management*, 7(4), 303–313.

Watty, R. (2013). Assumptions for incremental innovations in SMEs in International Conference on Engineering Design ICED 13, Seoul Korea, 19–22, August, 2013, ICED 13/262.

Wef, W. (2014). *The global competitiveness Report*. Geneva: World Economic Forum.

Weiser, P. J. (2011). Innovation, entrepreneurship, and the information age. *Journal on Telecommunications and High Technology Law*, 9, 1.

Wenger, E. C., and Snyder, W. M. (2000). Communities of practice: The organizational frontier. *Harvard Business Review*, 78(1), 139–146.

Wentz, R. (2010). Innovation Centre India: Innovation Machine Tata Motors Launches Disruptive Innovation Tata Nano. Where is Volkswagen?, The Innovation Machine, retrieved on 20 January 2011 from http://www.the-innovation-machine.com/?p=77

Wienstroth, F. (2013). BMW Group and UnternehmerTUM bring TechShop to Germany, Automobile manufacturer supports expansion of Entrepreneurship Centre at Technical University Munich (TUM).

Xie, X. M., Zeng, S. X., and Tam, C. M. (2010). Overcoming barriers to innovation in SMEs in China: A perspective based cooperation network. *Innovation*, 12(3), 298–310.

Zainol, F. A., Daud, W. N. W., Shamsu, L., Abubakar, H. S., and Halim, H. A. (2018). A linkage between entrepreneurial leadership and SMEs performance: An integrated review. *International Journal of Academic Research in Business and Social Sciences*, 8(4), 104–118.

Zheng, C. J. (2013). TechShop Partners with BMW Group and Unternehmer-TUM–Center for Innovation and Business Creation at Technical University Munich. Press Release. [Online] Available from http://www. techshop. ws/press_releases.html

# Index

addition 2, 3, 7, 15, 20, 34, 36, 37, 43, 45, 47, 48, 50, 53, 62, 66, 69, 70, 71, 82
Africa: direct investment 61; economic growth of 73; energy-efficient services 73; home growth 61; innovation barriers 36; innovation democracy 53; innovation development 48; natural resources of 45; policy formation 49; policymakers in 74; promoting innovation 22, 85; sustainable innovation 73
African communities 45
agricultural growth 75
agricultural land barrier 36
agricultural sector 65, 67
Air Canada 51
alliances 45–48, 51, 52, 87
Amazon 7
Ampex 65
anti-trust 32, 48
Apple Incorporation 19
Asia 73

Banking systems 7
barrier approach 34
barriers to innovation 30–33
biotechnology industry 46
BMW 87
bottom of the pyramid 9, 21
bottom-up solution 43
boundaryless cooperative relationship 42
bureaucracy 32, 35

business environment 3–5, 28, 30, 66, 81, 83
business framework 6
business innovation 2, 43
business problems 16
business techniques 5, 83

cannibalise 33
capital formation 35
Caterpillar Peoria 51
cheap goods and services 9
children approach 73
China 87
co-designing 72
collaboration 46, 49, 53, 55, 67, 73
commercial economy 86
commercialise grassroots innovation 71
commercialise technology 84
commercial profit 1
communication 15, 46, 83–84; concept of 41; effectiveness of 46
community development programmes 72
community workshops 72
competition 5, 16; concept of 66; economic development 80–82; globalisation of 66; importance of 8
competitive advantage 2–3, 5, 9, 23, 63, 67, 83
competitive environment 62
consumer market 65
conventional development programmes 62

conventional innovation systems 71
cooperative programme 35, 36
corporate level 2
corporate policy 15–16
corporate world 1
creative innovation concepts 47
creative methods 46
creative talents 15
creativity 14; entrepreneur 15; in
    individuals and organisations 15;
    in innovation development 21–24;
    successful outcomes 20–21
critical thinking 15
cross-functional innovation 42, 70
cross-organisational linkages 43
crowdfunding programmes 53
cultural goals 46
customers 42; business ecosystem
    43; incremental innovations 5;
    innovation process 44; needs of
    83; perspective of 48; product
    development 67; satisfaction
    and fulfilment of 80; service
    innovation 4–5, 47–48; strategic
    role of 4; transformation in 14;
    value of innovation 1–2, 4; webs of
    relationships 43

defence technology 36
democracy in innovation 75
demographics 63
development programme 22
Disney 7
disruptive innovation 3, 32, 35
distribution 47, 69

economic development 30, 80–82
economic growth 1, 5, 28, 73
economic performance 6, 63
economies of scale 47, 69
ecosystem 84
educational accomplishment 19
educational systems 22, 70
efficiency, enhancement of 5–6
employees 23
employment 19, 68–69
employment laws 36
energy-efficient services 73
Enterprise software (ERP) 31
entrepreneurial culture 72

entrepreneurial innovation 24
entrepreneurial personality 14, 15
entrepreneurship 19, 36, 62
Europe 9
experience 8, 9, 24, 43, 69
experimentation 22, 69, 72
external networks 49–50
extrinsic motivation 21

fabrication workshops 73
feedback concept 67–68
financial barriers 34
financial service industry 7
Finland 35
firm's capacity 22
formalise grassroots innovation 71
functional level 2

General Motors 87
global competitive environment 65
global innovation economy 74
globalisation 63, 72
Google 67
Government of Bangladesh 49
graduate programmes 73
grassroots innovation 71, 73;
    development of 73; Honey Bee
    Network model 45; innovation
    advancement 53; innovation
    democracy 75; strategic policy
    programmes 71

Hackerspaces 52, 53
high-quality community development
    skills 72
Honey Bee Network model 44, 45
horizontal network 43
human activity 8
human resources 85

ideas creation 16–18
income anticipation 34
incremental innovations 3, 5
India 44
ineffective innovation management
    system 20
information 42; and experience
    53; intrinsic motivation 21; and
    knowledge sharing 42; from social
    groups 20; visualisation of 24

innovation: advancement of 70, 73; assessment of 20; classifications of 4; competitive advantage 2–3; corporate level 2; in corporate world 1; definition of 1–2; framework 69; functional level 2; healthy requirement for 15; human activity 8; new business environment 3–5; service provision 4; technological innovation 5–8; value creation and development 1–2
innovation democracy 53, 75
innovation ecosystem 85, 86
innovation lab 85
innovation projects 30
innovation promotion 69; administrative skills 69; competitive advantage 67; culture importance 84; employment 68–69; feedback concept 67–68; innovation framework 69; innovation stakeholders 65–68; national innovation infrastructure 68; national innovation strategies 70; product design and development 66; stakeholders' engagement strategies 68–70
innovation stakeholders 65–68
innovation strategy 9
innovation theory 1
innovative culture 63
innovativeness 7, 9, 20, 80
innovative product 2, 4, 10, 46, 80; characteristic of 4
innovative talent: creativity 15–16; customers' transformation 14; ideas creation 16–18; imbibing creativity 24; innovation development 21–24; knowledge, significance of 18–20; successful outcomes 20–21; transformation process 18
inquisitiveness 15
instantaneous service 5
intellectual property 18, 71
intellectual property rights 44–45
internal innovations 44
international innovation policy framework 74

internet 6
intrinsic motivation 21
Israel 36

Japanese industries 3
Jobs, Steve 19

knowledge 9, 18–19, 68
knowledge architect 46
knowledge sharing 42, 84–86

labour force 7
leadership 68, 87
lean innovation 85
listening, act of 23
long-term sustainability 34
low income 9

macro-economic environment 74
Makerspaces 52, 53
managerial skills 69
market barrier/challenges 7, 32
market entry barriers 47
market environment 74
market failure 74
market globalisation 60
marketing innovation 4
mass production 69
material resources 85
Microsoft 8
mindset barriers 33
modern technologies 65
motivation 21, 22, 61
MYSQL (database software company) 6–7

national innovation strategies 68, 70
nation's innovation capacity 74
network and networking 42–43, 70
network cooperation 51
new business models 64
new pricing system 4
Nokia 42
non-physical asset 18
non-technological innovation 3–4

open innovation systems 17, 53, 84–86
opportunity 8, 17, 42, 69
Oracle 8

organisations 68; administrative capacity 31; bureaucracy 32, 35; competitive advantage 6; competitiveness of 2; external environment 7; foster grassroots innovation 72; intellectual asset of 18; managerial skills 69; mindset barriers 33; new methods implementation 3; potential resources 83; software transformation 8; teams and leaders of 70; time and money 22; transformation 16
overcoming barriers 28–37

partnerships strategies 52, 86–87
PayPal 7
*Paywith Square* 7
photography 8
Pixar 7
PlayStation idea 35
post-innovation returns 74
poverty 67
pre-action barriers concept 31
problem-solving approach 52, 73
problem-solving objectives 15
product design and development 32, 66
product innovation 45
production process 6
production system 69
product life cycle 16
proficient development 6

quality, concept of 80

regional development agencies 37
regulatory systems 70
relationship 68
Research and Development (R & D) network 49, 69
resource-based perspective 5
resources availability 86
resources, importance of 29–30
resources redistribution 16
responsibility/responsiveness 15, 29
revolutionary innovation 3
rural innovation concept 72

Sadbhav-SRISTI-Sanshodhan 75
Schumpeter, Joseph 1
self-confidence 19
self-effacing human resource knowledge 33
self-sufficient 20
service differentiation 5
service innovations 4–5, 8, 47, 60, 67, 83
Silicon Valley 8, 23, 50, 86
Singapore 73, 83
Singularity University (SU) 85
Skype 67
social sustenance 84
socioeconomic networks 43
software revolution 8
software transformation 8
solve problems 5, 15, 16, 21, 22, 46, 51, 52, 73
South Korea 73
speed 5, 67
stakeholders 80, 85; engagement strategies 68–70
Star Alliance partnership 51
strategic alliance 45
strategic architecture concept 83
strategic partnerships: communication 41; competitive advantage 45–48; engaging in networks 48–52; grassroots, innovation at 44–45; for innovation development 52–54; networks and knowledge 42–44
strategic policy programmes 71
strategic vertical alliance 45
strength-based motivation 21
success 62–65
successful outcomes 20–21
supporting innovation 71
sustainable innovation 73, 82
Sweden 20, 35
Swiss watch manufacturers 81–82
systematic approach 64

tactical design plan 83
talents development 16
Tata Group's Nano car 9
tax-based incentives 48
tax systems 70
technical innovation 4
technological innovations 33, 65

time and money resources 22
trade globalisation 83
transaction costs 9
transformation 7
transformational innovations 60, 61
transformation process 18, 86
transition movement network
   models 43
T-shaped model 23
21st century business costs 7

United States 87
universities 29, 37, 48, 49, 52,
   54, 55, 73, 85

value 67; of collaboration 46;
   concept of 6
value creating system 7
value creation 28
value of innovation 1–2, 4,
   64–65
vertical networks 43

*Walkman* 10
Walmart 66
water barrier 36
workforce skills 68